The Humanist and Non-Religious

Celebrant Handbook 2015

The Humanist and Non-Religious Celebrant Handbook
2015

A Comprehensive Guide to the Practice of Humanist and
Non-Religious Celebrancy and Officiating
within the United States of America.

Copyright ©Han Hills 2015

ISBN-10: 1508605726

ISBN-13: 978-1508605720

Disclaimer: Although every effort is made to ensure the information contained in this volume is correct at the time of publication, laws and public information are subject to regular change, and every reader is encouraged to pay attention to any changes made within their state or area. The author accepts no responsibility for discrepancies between the information contained within, and that held, or adopted, by any jurisdiction. The author is in no way responsible for the actions of any party taken as a result of the advice contained within this publication. The opinions given with regards to third party companies, organizations, or venders, are entirely those of the author. No payments, or other incentives, were received to recommend any organization over any other.

This book is dedicated to all the inspiring and imaginative professionals I have worked with over the years.

I would also like to thank the Humanist Institute for their hard work and encouragement.

Finally, but most importantly, I want to thank my wife for her many hours of support and patience.

Contents

Introduction — 1
Part One: The Role of the Celebrant — 3
- 1.1 - What is a Humanist or Non-Religious Celebrant? — 3
- 1.2 - The Meaning of your Title — 3
- 1.3 - What Types of Ceremony will you Perform? — 3
- 1.4 - Characteristics of a Humanist Ceremony — 4
- 1.5 - Practical Considerations — 5
- 1.6 - Your Writing Skills — 5
- 1.7 - Your Public Speaking Skills — 5
- 1.8 - Celebrant Dress and Clothing — 6
- 1.9 - Location and Travel — 6
- 1.10 - Seasonal Factors — 6
- 1.11 - Keeping a Calendar — 7
- 1.12 - Your Celebrant Boundaries and "Comfort Zone" — 7
- 1.13 - Maintaining your Reputation — 7
- 1.14 - Your Professional Ethic — 8
- 1.15 - Assessing your Celebrant Skills — 9

1.16 - Celebrant Skills Questionnaire — 10
1.17 - Understanding your Celebrant Skills Questionnaire Answers — 13

Part Two: Wedding Celebrations — 18
- 2.1 - Introducing Humanist and Non-Religious Weddings — 18
- 2.2 - What is a Humanist Wedding? — 18
- 2.3 - The Role of a Wedding Celebrant — 19
- 2.4 - Meeting with the Couple — 19
- 2.5 - The Key Players — 20
- 2.6 - Legal Ceremonies and Commitment Ceremonies — 20
- 2.7 - Same Sex Weddings — 20
- 2.8 - The "Cosmetic" Ceremony — 21
- 2.9 - Vow Renewals — 21
- 2.10 - Template Ceremonies — 22

2.11 - Relationship Biographies … 22
2.12 - Core Elements of a Wedding Ceremony … 22
- 2.12a - Processional … 22
- 2.12b - The "Presentation of the Bride" or "Giving Away" … 23
- 2.12c - Opening Words … 24
- 2.12d - Vows … 25
  - Recited or Self-Written Words … 25
  - Repeated Lines … 27
  - The "Putting of the Question" … 27
- 2.12e - Exchange of Rings … 28
- 2.12f - Closing Words … 28
- 2.12g - Pronouncements and Presentation … 29
- 2.12h - Recessional … 30

2.13 - The "Through Line" of the Ceremony … 30
2.14 - Ceremonial Music … 30
- Musical Interludes during the Ceremony … 31

2.15 - Photography … 31
2.16 - Additional Ceremonial Elements … 32
2.17 - Readings … 32
- Some Suggested Readings … 32

2.18 - Unity Ceremonies … 33
- 2.18a - Unity Candle … 34
- 2.18b - Sand Ceremony … 35
  - Three Vessels … 35
  - Family Sand Ceremony … 35
  - Beach Sand Ceremonies … 35
  - Hourglass Variation … 35
  - Hometown Earth Ceremony … 35
- 2.18c - Flower Ceremony … 36
  - Lei / Garland Ceremony … 36
- 2.18d - Knot Ceremonies … 36
  - Hand-fasting … 36
  - Fisherman's Knot … 36
  - Tying of the Braid … 36
- 2.18e - Wine Ceremony … 37
  - Wine and Chocolate Ceremony … 37
- 2.18f - Time Capsule … 37
- 2.18g - Water Ceremony … 37
  - Hand Wetting … 37
- 2.18h - Bread Breaking Ceremony … 37
- 2.18i - Coin Ceremony … 38

2.18j - Broom Jumping	38
2.18k - Oathing Stone	38
2.18l - Truce Bell	38
2.18m - Circling Ceremony	38
2.18n - The Seven Steps Ceremony	39
2.18o - Salt Ceremony	39
Indian Salt Ceremony	39
2.18p - Tree Planting Ceremony	39
2.18q - Unity Painting	40
2.18r - Tile Breaking Ceremony	40
2.18s - Unity Volcano	40
2.19 - Children and Wedding Ceremonies	40
Children as Participants	40
Children as Guests	41
2.20 - The Wedding Rehearsal	41
2.21 - Running a Wedding Rehearsal	43
2.22 - On the Day	45
2.23 - Understanding your Legal Obligations	45
2.24 - Wedding Cancellations	46
2.25 - Pre-Marital Education	46
2.26 - Dealing with a Crisis	47
2.27 - Understanding and Responding to Spiritual Differences	47
2.28 - Your Celebrant Kit	48
2.29 - Your Wedding Day Book	48
2.30 - Getting Paid	48
2.31 - Networking	49
2.32 - Knowing When to Exit	49
2.33 - Post Ceremony Follow-Up	49

Part Three: Funerals and Memorials   53

3.1 - Humanist and Non-Religious Funerals and Memorials	53
3.2 - What is a Humanist Memorial?	53
3.3 - The Difference between "In Need" and "Pre-Planning"	54
3.4 - In Need Preparation	54
The Initial Contact	54
Pricing	55
Contract	55

The Consulting Interview	55
3.5 - Pre-Planning with the Living	**56**
The Initial Contact	57
Pricing	57
Contract	57
The Consulting Interview	57
Completing the Process	58
3.6 - Core Elements of a Memorial	**58**
3.6a - Opening Words	58
3.6b - Personal Statements and Recollections	58
3.6c - Pre-Planned Recollections	59
3.6d - Spontaneous Statements	59
3.6e - Music	59
3.6f - Readings	60
3.6g - A Moment of Silence	60
3.7 - Ceremonial Additions	**60**
3.8 - On the Day	**61**

Part Four: Other Celebrations — 63

4.1 - Baby Naming and New Life Celebrations	**63**
4.1a - Core Elements of a New Life Ceremony	63
The Welcome	63
Announcing the Name	63
Parent's Promises	63
Guide Parent's Promises	63
The Closing	64
4.1b - Possible Additions to a New Life Ceremony	64
4.1c - How Much to Charge for a New Life Ceremony	64
4.2 - Invocations	**64**
Defining a Humanist Invocation	64
Gathering Information for the Invocation	65
What an Invocation is NOT	65
Pricing an Invocation	65
4.3 - Humanist and Non-Religious Blessings	**65**
Festive Blessings	65
Dinner Blessings	66
4.4 - Dedications	**66**
4.5 - Pet Funerals	**66**

Part Five: Building a Celebrant Business — 67

- 5.1 - Introduction to the Celebrant Business — 67
- 5.2 - Your State's Celebrant Requirements — 67
- 5.3 - Becoming "Ordained" — 67
- 5.4 - State Registration — 68
- 5.5 - Know your Marriage Laws — 68
- 5.6 - Tax and Small Business Law — 68
- 5.7 - Recording Sales, Expenses, and Earnings — 68
- 5.8 - Services, Pricing, and Payments — 69
  - Choosing your Services — 69
  - Setting Prices — 69
  - Taking Payments — 69
  - Your Contract — 69
- 5.9 - Choosing a Business Name — 70
  - Should you use the Name of a Town or State in your Business Name? — 70
  - Does your Name Roll Off the Tongue in an Appealing and Memorable Way? — 70
  - Should your Name be Descriptive? — 70
  - Is the DBA Available? — 70
  - Is a Friendly and Catchy Domain Name Available? — 70
- 5.10 - Online Marketing — 71
  - Creating a Website — 71
  - Social Media — 71
  - Professional Wedding Site Marketing — 71
  - Blogging — 71
- 5.11 - Offline Marketing — 71
  - Networking — 71
  - Printed Materials — 72
  - Mailings — 72
- 5.12 - Building your Professional Kit — 72
  - Clothing — 72
  - Tools of the Trade — 73
- 5.13 - Working with Clients — 73
  - Your Service Questionnaires — 73
  - Meeting Locations — 73
- 5.14 - Continuing Growth — 73
  - Building your Skills — 73
  - Sharing your Experiences — 74
- 5.15 - New Celebrant Business Checklist — 75

Appendix A: Wedding Celebrant Laws by State	**77**
Appendix B: Wedding License Rules by U.S. State	**89**
Appendix C: Glossary of Wedding Terms	**151**
Appendix D: Glossary of Funeral and Memorial Terms	**161**
Appendix E: Sample Wedding Questionnaire	**167**
Appendix F: Sample Memorial Questionnaire	**171**
Appendix G: Example Contract / Information Form	**177**
Appendix H: Further Resources	**181**
Afterword	**185**

Introduction

The twenty first century has seen an astonishing rise in the popularity of ceremonies that break with tradition. Couples are choosing weddings which are primarily designed reflect their story and style. People reaching the end of life are looking to celebrate their past in ways which respect their legacy.

This new era calls forth the need for a new type of Celebrant, a new master of ceremonies, and trained official, who is qualified to guide this new kind of celebration.

Although our cultures and societies change, there will always be a need for family and community to mark the great milestones in life. Increasingly, there is a desire to celebrate these special days in a very personal and human way, without the necessity for the traditions and restrictions of faith or religion.

This need requires a vastly increased number of skilled professional Celebrants across the country. The hope in writing this handbook is to give new, and developing, Humanist and Non-Religious Celebrants advice, and guidelines, on making every job they do one they, and their clients, will be proud of.

The book is divided into five main parts, with many appendices of reference information. Each part gives practical advice on performing your Celebrant role.

Unlike almost all books on Humanist ceremonies in the past, I have devoted few pages to examples. The reason for this is twofold. Firstly, with a little guidance and ingenuity thousands of examples can be found online, and we give many references at the end of the book. Secondly, the drive behind a modern ceremony is creativity. We should not be looking to repeat what has come before but rather to expand our repertoire in every direction. We are not constrained by tradition when building our celebrations. We are creating the ceremonies of tomorrow.

The reader will have noticed that this book is aimed at celebrants who may describe themselves as either Humanist or Non-religious. Although many may be comfortable adopting both these terms, there are, of course, a significant number of non-religious people who may feel uncomfortable adopting the title of Humanist. However, almost all ceremonies which might be classed primarily as Non-religious have a strong underpinning of Humanist values. These include empathy, notions of equality, an emphasis on the natural basis of existence, as well as any others. For this reason, I hope the reader will forgive my tendency to frequently use these terms interchangeably, or in concert.

I hope you enjoy this book, and that even the most seasoned Celebrant will find something new to consider as they progress through its pages.

Part One: The Role of the Celebrant

In this section we will introduce the role of the Celebrant and the key skills and talents that make up the foundation of the part we play in celebrations and ceremonies.

1.1 - What is a Humanist or Non-Religious Celebrant?

A Humanist or Non-Religious Celebrant is a qualified, usually experienced, professional who helps individuals, couples, families, and communities create and perform ceremonies that recognize and celebrate important events, milestones, and values. They do this in ways which reflect purely human values and thinking.

Let us take time to break down what we mean by these statements and terms, so you can fully understand the role you will be entrusted to play.

1.2 - The Meaning of your Title

Why do we use the word Celebrant? Although this is the most common term we adopt for ourselves, many of those practicing use the term interchangeably with others, such as Officiant, or Minister. Let's briefly compare these definitions to understand how each may be appropriate.

Celebrant: a person who performs, or leads, a religious ceremony.

Officiant: one (as a priest) who officiates at a religious rite.

Minister: a person whose job involves leading church services, performing religious ceremonies (such as marriages), and providing spiritual, or religious, guidance to other people.

At its core the title Celebrant is perhaps most accurate for the role we expect to take as we start to practice. However, your choice of title can involve subtle factors beyond the raw definition.

There are many levels to the public understanding of terms and titles. You may encounter individuals for whom words such as Celebrant, and Officiant, cause confusion. This can be less so with the title of Minister.

The choice of title you choose, whether in general or for particular events, is ultimately your decision. It is important, however, that you do not mislead others as to your professional, or educational, status. You should also undertake your duties in a manner which carefully, and consistently, reflects Humanist philosophy and practice.

1.3 - What Types of Ceremony will you perform?

As a practicing Celebrant, you should expect the majority of your duties to involve the preparation and performance of weddings. The officiating, also known as solemnizing, of a marriage is one of the few ceremonies in the United States for which there are specific legal requirements. These can vary greatly between states. Appendix A of this volume lists the current marriage Celebrant requirements for each state. It is important that you are familiar with the rules in the region you practice. You should also pay close attention to any changes in local laws.

In addition to weddings, there are many other types of ceremony you may be asked to perform. These include, but are not limited to: funerals or memorial services, new life ceremonies, commonly referred to as "Baby Namings", and invocations, or formal statements, which begin many public events. There may be other requests for ceremonial roles specific to your skills, organizational positions, and experience.

1.4 - Characteristics of a Humanist Ceremony

Humanist and Non-religious ceremonies already make up a significant percentage of the weddings taking place in Northern Europe and are fast taking hold across the United States. Traditionally, ceremonial practices were restricted to the policies, and requirements, of a particular faith or denomination. An Officiant was required, by the rules of a church, to devote large amounts of their ceremony to prayers, and scripture, increasingly unrelated to the personal lives and experiences of those involved, and these would often also be notably out of touch with the reality of the beliefs and perspectives of the couple.

A Humanist ceremony, in large part, does away with these restrictions and outdated requirements. With these ceremonies, there is no need to reference ancient texts and clerical demands. The day is truly one for the individuals, couples, families, and communities to build. Although these ceremonies are free from scripture and the supernatural, they very often incorporate other aspects of cultural tradition. This can be most easily seen in the structure, and specific elements, of the wedding ceremony. Almost all will contain an exchange of vows and rings. Couples from particularly specific cultural backgrounds may choose to incorporate symbolic traditions appropriate to those. One example might be where a secular Jewish couple choose to include the well known "glass breaking" at the conclusion of their wedding.

A Humanist ceremony is a celebration of life, even when recognizing the natural role of death. These ceremonies focus on the lives of the people at their center. This may be a couple entering wedlock, a person ending their life, or one whose life is just beginning. They may also be representative of a group of people making a difference to their local community.

As a Humanist Celebrant, you represent the philosophy and outlook of Humanism. You may be regularly required to give explanations, both brief and detailed, of Humanist thinking and practice. It is important, in such situations, to have a comfortable familiarity with the key points of Humanism. You should be able to convey these quickly and clearly to strangers and groups. I encourage you to read the "Humanism and Its Aspirations" document, created and published by the American Humanist Association, and freely available on their web site, AmericanHumanist.org. It is worth taking time to learn and practice discussing the Humanist approach to life. You may wish to try out your explanations on family and friends. As with every aspect of your ceremony preparation, those close to you can often give you valuable, and sometimes unexpected, feedback.

1.5 - Practical Considerations

Much has been written about the "philosophy" of the Humanist, or Non-religious, ceremony. It is vital to understand, however, that the role of the officiant is primarily a *practical* one. What follows are some practical factors to which you should give important consideration.

1.6 - Your Writing Skills

Although many Celebrants rely heavily on material taken from the many sources available, both online and offline, the creation of a truly unique, and personalized, ceremony absolutely requires some ability in composition. You do not have to be a Pulitzer standard author, however, to create a ceremony all those attending will remember fondly.

I recommend reading as many ceremonies as you can, when starting out on your career in celebration. You will find a wide variation in style. The best writing comes from a clear sincerity. Write in the way you feel most comfortable, while maintaining a respect, and air of modern formality, in your material.

Most importantly, when composing a ceremony you should remember that you are writing text to be *read aloud*, rather than silently from the page. Keep you sentences clear and concise, and use simpler and shorter words where possible. Read your work aloud to yourself, or a friend, and change anything which sounds clumsy or over complicated. Teach yourself to become familiar with the language of ceremonies. I have created glossaries of terms, for both weddings and memorials, later in this book.

There are huge numbers of ceremony examples available in book form, and online, as well as many widely available video examples. If you study a broad range of these, you should quickly find a style which suits your personality.

Another important factor in composing a ceremony is to consider your audience. There are some groups for which a simpler language is more appropriate, while others may expect, and indeed prefer, something a little more formal, or literary in construction. If you can adapt to the needs of each occasion, you will please your clients far more than if you stick to a rigidly defined style and format.

1.7 - Your Public Speaking Skills

The role of the Celebrant is one of performance. You will be expected to speak in front of large groups and should be comfortable doing so. Additionally, you should cultivate a clear and strong speaking voice. Although some venues will provide microphone amplification many will not. There are practical, and entertaining, written guides to improving your public speaking skills, but there is no substitute for practice and receiving personal feedback. You may want to try out your skills on friends and family, or perhaps offer to give talks to a local group or club.

Breath technique is essential for proper voice projection. Whereas, in normal speech, one may use air from the top of the lungs, a correctly projected voice uses air properly flowing from the expansion of the diaphragm. In good vocal technique, well-balanced respiration is especially important to maintaining vocal projection. The goal is to isolate and relax the muscles controlling the vocal folds, so that they are unimpaired by tension.

I have included some recommended guides to improving your public speaking skills at the end of this book. Remember, though, practice is essential.

1.8 - Celebrant Dress and Clothing

There are no traditional Humanist Celebrant costumes or robes. Most simply choose to dress smartly to suit the occasion. For men, suits, vests, and ties are often the standard. For women, a tasteful dress, or gown, is often appropriate. It is important to maintain a clean and respectable appearance at all times and not to choose a style, or color, which will distract from the atmosphere or focus of the occasion.

In representing Humanism, some Celebrants choose to wear a "Happy Humanist" lapel pin, or perhaps go as far as to wear a stole, a ceremonial cloth draped over the shoulders bearing a Humanist insignia. For some the use of symbolism, or raiment, can be felt inappropriate or outside their zone of comfort.

This can be one area where it can be useful to consult the client. An individual, couple, or family may have strong opinions on what they expect you to wear, and they too may be uncomfortable with garments which seem a little too traditionally religious.

It has been mentioned to me, by several female Celebrants, that the addition of a single plain stole can help to establish, and emphasize, their importance and authority in the ceremonial proceedings.

Tip: Ask the client what colors they have chosen for their event. You can then be sure not to wear items which clash.

1.9 - Location and Travel

Even if you live in a high population area, such as a major city, you may well be asked to travel wider distances to perform ceremonies. It is important to consider the availability of transport and how far you are willing to travel on any particular day. Long drives, plus the performing of a ceremony, can be tiring. Additionally, some of you may feel uncomfortable driving at night or in twilight. It is important to account for this when deciding whether to accept a booking.

When starting out in your Celebrant practice, you should examine a map of the region surrounding your "base of operations", and decide on the areas, and distances, you will be happy to cover. Not only will this affect the bookings you take, but this will also impact the methods, and locations, in which you market your services.

1.10 - Seasonal Factors

Weddings will likely make up the majority of the ceremonies you are asked to perform. It is important to realize that these will be highly seasonal, in terms of booking volumes, and dependant on climate and public holidays. The peak months for wedding ceremonies are usually between April and October, though in warmer climates this can extend further into the winter months. In particularly hot climates, you may find a slight dip in bookings around July and August, especially where clients tend to plan an outdoor ceremony. Extended periods in the sun can be uncomfortable, especially when dressed in formal wear. Heat can also take an extra toll on the very young and the very old.

There are times throughout the year when more couples will be looking to plan their wedding day. You should expect enquiries peak just after New Year and again around Valentine's Day.

For other types of ceremony there is no annual season to speak of. You can expect to take bookings for Memorials, or New Life ceremonies, at any time of the year.

1.11 - Keeping a Calendar

When working as a Celebrant your calendar becomes vital. It will be used not only for planning bookings but also for anticipating your own important life events, and commitments, many months in advance. Although it is most important to record coming ceremonial events, and to avoid any possibility of double bookings, you will need to mark off your own vacations and other key personal factors. Seasonally, you may need to plan your vacations outside your busiest months. Ideally, you should have a calendar to hand at all times, perhaps installed on your phone, so that you will know immediately your availability for any date and time. An excellent tool is Google Calendar (available with any Gmail account), which can synchronize between a phone and computer, and also allows for multiple users.

Tip: When noting a booking on your calendar, be sure to account for preparation and travel. When considering more than one booking on a day it is vital to know if a transition from one to the next is viable.

1.12 - Your Celebrant Boundaries and "Comfort Zone"

If you have been requested to perform a particular ceremony it is almost certain that the primary parties want the occasion to be Humanist, or Non-religious, in nature. This position may well be held regardless of the spiritual or faith views taken by others attending. However, on occasion you may be asked to include "spiritual elements".

Whether you agree to take up an offer to officiate, and how you negotiate with those requesting such a ceremony, can be a matter of boundaries. Many Humanist Celebrants are uncomfortable with, and unwilling to allow, any notions of, or references to, spirituality of any kind in their ceremonies. Others may allow some reference, providing it does not misrepresent or distort the core principles and message of the ceremony. A good rule of thumb is to never participate in anything which is insincere or hypocritical. If you are honest, and true to your own philosophical position, you can't go far wrong. It is important to carefully consider your boundaries before you begin practicing. Such questions will arise sooner rather than later.

1.13 - Maintaining your Reputation

As a respected figure at any event, and with an important role as an ambassador of Humanism, it is critical that you look to maintain your reputation at all times. Only through having a good reputation will you successfully build your Celebrant business. It is an accepted statistic that 95% of couples choosing their wedding officiant online do so according to reviews and testimonials. One bad review can undo the work of a hundred excellent reviews, so be certain to carefully cultivate and encourage feedback when you feel you have given good service.

1.14 - Your Professional Ethic

The position and responsibility of the Celebrant requires a strong professional ethic. I believe that there is a code all professionals should follow. In my own work I have created a set of rules I try very hard to follow. You may wish to adopt some, or all, of these.

1. Treat everyone with dignity, respect and politeness at all times.

2. *Do not swear.* The use of vulgar language is not only offensive but insults the dignity of your position.

3. *Do not drink.* Many ceremonial occasions involve the large consumption of alcohol, often with regrettable consequences. As the Celebrant you are acting in a professional capacity and must maintain decorum at all times. There will be occasions where clients are quite insistent that you join them in a drink. There is no harm in a polite refusal; in fact that is always the very best policy.

4. *Do not "fraternize".* Although it is important to be friendly, always be aware of the interpersonal boundaries which exist between you and clients or guests. As a figure of authority, there may be occasions where you receive personal advances from those you encounter. Days of celebration are very emotional occasions. Any advances, or intimate suggestions, you receive should always be politely, but firmly, declined.

5. *Do not smoke.* Strangely, this is a rule some other Celebrants of my acquaintance have contested, and this is ultimately a matter of personal choice. However, smoking is now a minority practice, which many consider unpleasant and also undignified. The dignity of your position is not something you should sacrifice, and, for the smokers among you, I strongly recommend waiting until you have finished your duties and left the venue.

6. *Do not discuss politics.* Political opinions vary widely and can often be extremely emotive. Discussion of these topics can often lead to negative conflict. As a professional, hired to officiate and oversee a ceremony in a dignified way, you should avoid engaging in such debates or being seen to take personal positions which some may find offensive. This is a rule all should follow in any workplace, unless hired as a pundit.

7. *Do not debate religion.* While this is almost certainly a topic on which you will have strong opinions, it can be extremely unwise to engage in fervent debate on religious matters whilst acting in your professional capacity. Much as with politics, these can be extremely emotive issues. Although the ceremonies you will be asked to perform may be non-religious or humanistic in nature, it is almost certain that some guests, or attendees, will hold different spiritual outlooks to yourself. It should be your primary concern not to cause any offense among people you encounter in your capacity as a Celebrant, however much you may find yourself personally aggrieved by any viewpoint your hear expressed.

8. *Ensure you are always punctual.* Many ceremonies are very carefully timed and you will be critical to proceedings. Arriving when you have agreed is essential in order to facilitate a successful day. As a Celebrant, I always consider it good practice to plan to arrive slightly earlier than is needed.

This planning allows for any unexpected traffic while travelling and also gives you time to address any unexpected problems you may encounter at the venue prior to the beginning of the proceedings.

9. *There is no such thing as "Off Duty".* From the time you arrive at the venue, to the time you depart, you are acting in the capacity of a professional. Particularly during weddings, you may be encouraged to greatly relax. To do so can put you in danger of acting in an unprofessional manner. This may then have a catastrophic effect on your reputation in the following days.

10. *Discretion is critical.* It is unprofessional to share sensitive information about your clients or the ceremony. Where you share the details of an event, either with other Celebrants or friends and very especially online, you should not refer to real names and dates unless you are given very specific permission to do so by the clients. I have performed weddings where the ceremony was held in a very deliberately private way often for sensitive personal reasons. It is important to respect these confidences at all times.

11. *Keep a smart appearance.* Your image is a key part of your professionalism and should be maintained at all times. You should ensure that your garments are clean and that you have a tidy appearance. In my own practice as an officiant, I do not loosen my tie, or adjust my clothes for comfort, until I am finally away from the venue. Your clients will hugely respect this sort of professional behavior.

12. *Do not overstep your role.* In your capacity as a Celebrant you will have many different duties to perform. It is important, however, not to infringe on the roles, or duties, of the other professionals you will work beside. Remain aware of who has been hired to perform specific duties, and allow them to do so without criticism or obstruction. You should resist the temptation to "step in" if you feel another vendor of participant is not performing as you would choose or expect. Such actions rarely result in the best resolution to any problem.

13. *Do not proselytize.* You should never use your position as officiant to promote your own personal viewpoint or agenda.

Always remember that your reputation is your greatest asset. Your behavior will make or break that reputation, something it can take a long time to build but only a single careless moment to destroy.

1.15 - Assessing your Celebrant Skills

When starting out as a Celebrant, it is important to be aware of, and understand, your personal strengths and weaknesses in that role. With frank self-assessment you should be able to highlight areas for growth and improvement. You will also be able to understand the special and unique qualities which you bring to the role and those which can be used to promote your business and practice. What follows is a set of questions relating to the skills best required to practice and succeed as a Humanist or Non-religious Celebrant. There are no right or wrong answers. This is merely an exercise to help you analyze your strengths and weaknesses. Afterwards I have given a commentary on each question to further help you understand their importance. Please circle your own self-assessed rating based on a number from one to ten.

1.16 - Celebrant Skills Questionnaire

1. How familiar are you with Humanism?

(1 – Not at all | 10 – Very familiar)

1   2   3   4   5   6   7   8   9   10

2. Have you any previous experience as a Celebrant?

(1 – No experience | 10 – Extensive experience)

1   2   3   4   5   6   7   8   9   10

3. Have you any previous experience as a Public Speaker?

(1 – No experience | 10 – Extensive experience)

1   2   3   4   5   6   7   8   9   10

4. Are you nervous speaking in front of others?

(1 – Very nervous | 10 – Extremely comfortable)

1   2   3   4   5   6   7   8   9   10

5. Do you have a strong and clear speaking voice?

(1 – Very quiet | 10 – Strong and clear / Theatrical)

1   2   3   4   5   6   7   8   9   10

6. Do you have good writing skills?

(1 – Very limited | 10 – Professional writing experience)

1   2   3   4   5   6   7   8   9   10

7. Do you have a clean and smart appearance?

(1 – Very relaxed / rough appearance | 10 – Extremely smart at all times)

1   2   3   4   5   6   7   8   9   10

8. Can you remain standing for several hours at a time?

(1 – Poor physical condition | 10 – Excellent physical condition)

1   2   3   4   5   6   7   8   9   10

9. Are you comfortable travelling?

(1 – Dislike or are unable to travel far | 10 – Excellent and comfortable traveler)

1   2   3   4   5   6   7   8   9   10

10. Are you comfortable with large groups or strangers?

(1 – Very Uncomfortable | 10 – Completely at ease)

1   2   3   4   5   6   7   8   9   10

11. Can you keep your composure in a crisis?

(1 – Easily panicked | 10 – Consistently calm)

1   2   3   4   5   6   7   8   9   10

12. Are you methodical and organized?

(1 – Chaotic and disorganized | 10 – Fastidious and highly organized)

1   2   3   4   5   6   7   8   9   10

13. Can you work flexible hours and weekends?

(1 – Very restricted hours | 10 – Flexible 24/7)

1   2   3   4   5   6   7   8   9   10

14. Can you commit to bookings months in advance?

(1 – Cannot pre-plan | 10 – Can plan a year in advance)

1   2   3   4   5   6   7   8   9   10

15. Do you have any small business or bookkeeping experience?

(1 – No experience at all | 10 – Extensive experience)

1   2   3   4   5   6   7   8   9   10

16. How familiar are you with web design or creation?

(1 – No experience at all | 10 – Extensive experience)

1   2   3   4   5   6   7   8   9   10

17. How familiar are you with online social networking?

(1 – No experience at all | 10 – Extensive experience)

1   2   3   4   5   6   7   8   9   10

18. Are you good at talking on the telephone?

(1 – Dislike telephones | 10 – Very comfortable)

1   2   3   4   5   6   7   8   9   10

19. Can you organizer you calendar or schedule?

(1 – Very poor planner | 10 – Excellent planner)

1   2   3   4   5   6   7   8   9   10

20. Have you attended many weddings?

(1 – None | 10 – Dozens of different types)

1   2   3   4   5   6   7   8   9   10

21. Have you attended many funerals or memorials?

(1 – None | 10 – Dozens of different types)

1   2   3   4   5   6   7   8   9   10

22. How large do you plan building your Celebrant business?

(1 – One ceremony only | 10 – Full time professional)

1   2   3   4   5   6   7   8   9   10

1.17 - Understanding your Celebrant Skills Questionnaire

1. How familiar are you with Humanism?

It is important to be familiar with Humanism, how Humanists view the world, and the ethical principles they follow. Even the most non-religious ceremonies reflect a Humanistic outlook to some degree. Humanist principles are important; not only in learning how to construct and perform your ceremonies but also as to how you should behave as a Celebrant, and explain your outlook to others. Many people you encounter at an event will be curious, or perhaps confused, as to your religious outlook, and some will have very negative preconceptions given to them by other religious figures. It is important to have a clear and positive explanation of your own spiritual outlook to hand. Understand what Humanism is, not simply what it stands opposed to. Have your "elevator speech", a two or three sentence snappy summary of the key points, prepared and practiced.

2. Have you any previous experience as a Celebrant?

You may already have officiated ceremonies, perhaps for friends or in another country. You may be reading this with a desire to take your celebrancy to a new level. If so, you have already taken a key step. It is important to remember that every ceremony will present its own challenges, and that the nature of Humanist ceremonies is that they are extremely responsive to the needs of a couple or the individual. Like most professions, celebrancy requires a degree of continuing study and practice. However many ceremonies you perform, you should keep an open mind about the new challenges ahead.

3. Have you any previous experience as a Public Speaker?

The ability to speak in public is a core skill for any Celebrant. It takes practice but can be developed in many ways. Clubs and discussion groups are a great way to stretch, and to refine, your presentation skills. I have listed some recommended reading on this subject later in this book.

4. Are you nervous speaking in front of others?

When performing a ceremony, you will need to focus your concentration on many aspects other than your own nerves. As with question three, there are many ways to develop your ability to talk confidently in public. As a Celebrant, you will have to give a convincing appearance of calm. Many will be looking to you as the professional center of the proceedings.

5. Do you have a strong and clear speaking voice?

As a Celebrant, you will perform at many events with attendance well into double or triple figures. In some cases, especially when an event is held outdoors, you will not have the benefit of a microphone or amplification. It is advisable to practice your vocal skills, and adopt theatrical voice techniques such as correct breathing and projection.

Tip: When planning to officiate at a venue, it is worth considering whether you will need the aid of amplification. The bigger the audience, the more volume you will need. If the venue is outdoors, especially on a beach, you will be competing with a great deal of ambient noise. Even with a strong voice and good projection skills, the more effort you have to put into volume the less energy you will have for the expression, and intonation, of your words. If a DJ is working the ceremony, they may be able to supply a microphone. The best type of microphone for most occasions is a wireless lapel unit.

6. Do you have good writing skills?

A key aspect of Humanist ceremonies is that they do not adhere to a rigid, or prescribed, format and text. Even if you borrow aspects of your ceremonies from other sources, there will be times when you must write new materials, or adapt significant parts of your ceremony to the occasion. Understanding the difference between good and bad writing, and having the confidence to write, becomes extremely important. You should also understand that you are writing words to be *spoken*, rather than read silently from a page. This makes it all the more important that you keep your writing clear, and simple, and give it an easy and comfortable rhythm.

7. Do you have a clean and smart appearance?

There is a strong expectation that a professional Celebrant will have an excellent standard of appearance. Personal hygiene, neat and tidy hair and nails, clean and pressed clothing, often dry cleaned, and polished shoes, are expected and important. Elaborate personal adornment can be an unwanted distraction during a ceremony and should ideally be kept to a minimum or covered. It is important always to understand that you should not be the primary focus of the occasion. That privilege belongs to those for whom you are performing the ceremony.

8. Can you remain standing for several hours at a time?

Before, during, and after a ceremony, you can find yourself on your feet for several hours at a time. This may sometimes be in very warm surroundings or in direct sunlight. If this is a potential problem, you should consider that before accepting Celebrant bookings. This should also be something to consider when choosing clothing and footwear. Shoes can be smart and polished while also built for comfort.

9. Are you comfortable travelling?

Many ceremonies may be some distance from your home. It is important to be realistic about the distance you can travel to and from an event on any single day. Many people are uncomfortable driving long distances in twilight or in darkness. For ceremonies held later in the day, you may find yourself returning home at night, and this should be considered when deciding whether to accept a booking. For more distant ceremonies, where an overnight stay is required, the client should be willing to lodge you in comfortable conditions. In all circumstances, where you incur noticeable travel costs, you should look for reimbursement. The 2015 I.R.S. prescribed business travel compensation rate is $0.575 per mile. Do not forget to calculate your cost for the return journey in addition to your travel to the venue.

10. Are you comfortable with large groups or strangers?

Many people are uncomfortable in crowds. At weddings and memorials you will almost always find yourself surrounded by large groups of people. This is something you should find becomes easier with practice. Breathe slowly, talk about neutral subjects, and try to keep smiling. If you are uncomfortable shaking hands, you may want to take a small bottle of hand sanitizer to use discretely.

11. Can you keep your composure in a crisis?

Celebrations such as weddings and funerals can be socially complex and emotional. The unexpected *will* happen, and often the Celebrant, perceived as an experienced professional and leader, may be required to take charge and resolve problems. At such times, the ability to remain calm is a true asset. However, it is also important to understand that taking the helm may not always be the right move. In some situations the best response is to step aside, and let others, better placed and suited, resolve an issue.

12. Are you methodical and organized?

Organization is a hugely important skill for a Celebrant. The more bookings you accept the more critical this becomes. You should ensure your calendar is kept accurate and up to date. You will need to create files of information, for clients and events, which are always easy to locate. You will need to plan to have your clothing, and other essential items, ready for the day and to leave home in good time to reach any venue. Where your skills in this area may be lacking, it can be helpful to ask for assistance from somebody close and reliable to help you create your organizational methods and processes.

For any Celebrant taking more than a few bookings a year their calendar becomes an essential tool. For safety, I recommend using an electronic calendar stored online, such as that freely available on Google. A more traditional paper organizer can work well if you keep it to hand, but you should always have a back up copy of your booking information, stored in a separate location.

13. Can you work flexible hours and weekends?

You may be asked to perform ceremonies at all times of the day and on any day of the week. Weekends are especially popular for weddings, and memorials are often planned to coincide with mealtimes. If you have other employment, or family obligations, it is important to carefully consider these when building your Celebrant business and choosing to accept bookings. Wedding celebrancy also necessitates a highly seasonal commitment. The high workload in summer months may have an impact on your ability to take vacations, or other trips, during those times.

14. Can you commit to bookings months in advance?

Although funerals and memorials usually happen within a short number of days of the booking, wedding bookings can be requested as much as a year in advance. Although events that far in the future can be unpredictable, it is important to consider what other factors may affect your life over such a period. If you are planning to move house, or take retirement, you may want to consider a "cut-off date" for taking bookings in a particular location or in significant volumes.

15. Do you have any small business or bookkeeping experience?

As a professional Celebrant, you will be working in a *business* capacity. You will be contracting for work, taking payments, and incurring expenses. You should ensure that you fulfill all legal obligations and observe the best business practices. It is especially important to understand your obligations with regards to tax. If you have limited experience in accounting you may want to seek some friendly professional advice. There are many reasonably priced accountants in every city, and a little of their time could save you many hours of frustration, head-scratching, cost, and worry.

16. How familiar are you with web design or creation?

We live in the Internet age. If you plan on any level of marketing, an online presence is *essential*. A web site, which showcases your services and skills, can be fairly easy to set up using tools such as WordPress. As with accountants, there are many reasonably priced professionals you may wish to turn to for advice. When looking to hire a professional, such as an accountant or designer, an excellent way to start is to ask friends and associates for their recommendations of those they have had success working with.

When choosing a name for your business you should also consider the domain name, or Internet address, that you might use. Check that the domain you wish to use is available before making a firm commitment. You will be a "for profit" entity, so the suffix *.com* is more appropriate than .org, which is the one usually adopted by non-profit organizations.

17. How familiar are you with online social networking?

In addition to your web site, it is useful to become familiar with social networks, such as Facebook and LinkedIn. Not only are these proven, and highly affordable, ways to promote your business, but they are also a way to network with other Celebrants for the purpose of sharing ideas, information, and experience.

18. Are you good at talking on the telephone?

Along with e-mail, you will almost certainly take enquiries by telephone. This can be a vital chance to make a first impression. Your vocal qualities are one of the important factors clients will consider before booking your services. It can be useful to have a questionnaire by the phone, to ensure you collect all the important information during the conversation. I have included sample enquiry forms, and also questionnaires, later in this book.

19. Have you attended many weddings?

The best way to learn about weddings is to attend them. Ceremonies can differ radically in style. In watching how the various roles fit together, and witnessing the emotions and reactions of those involved, you will find yourself far more prepared for the experiences you will encounter when officiating. I strongly advise against becoming a "wedding crasher", but do look out for family, friends, or colleagues, who may be very happy for you to attend their own ceremony. You can also find many wedding videos available online, and these allow you to observe without intruding, dressing formally, or having to eat any poorly catered dinners.

20. Have you attended many funerals or memorials?

As with weddings, you cannot fully appreciate funerals or memorials unless you have some personal experience of the formalities and emotions involved. Unlike weddings, funerals can sometimes be easier to attend without an invitation. Many ceremonies make allowance for a number of unexpected, or "walk-in", mourners. You should, of course, exercise caution and discretion in attending any event uninvited, and never fail to have respect for the occasion and those emotionally involved. As a substitute for attending in person, there are also videos and documentaries on this subject available online.

21. How large do you plan building your Celebrant business?

How greatly you intend to develop your Celebrant practice is entirely your decision. Some Celebrants only practice a single ceremony, while others may limit themselves to just a few ceremonies in any year, and then for only family or friends.

For those looking to build a professional celebrancy practice, these can be developed into a full business bringing in a fairly reasonable income, especially in summer months. As a professional, you will almost certainly find that weddings will make up the the bulk of your bookings, and this will likely be the area on which you focus your primary marketing strategy. As with any business venture, the more effort you put in the more rewards, and success, you will see. Celebrancy is not a "get rich quick" scheme by any means but a profession which can give tremendous fulfillment, and fun, in addition to a pay packet every time you perform. Success is absolutely there for you to find, if you plan carefully, and truly enjoy your work.

Part Two: Wedding Celebrations

2.1 - Introducing Humanist and Non-Religious Weddings

As a Humanist or Non-Religious Celebrant, weddings will probably make up the vast majority of the ceremonies you perform. Mirroring trends in Northern Europe, the demand for marriage ceremonies of this type is growing at an increasing rate across the United States. This is particularly true among the younger generations, many of whom now identify as non-believers or consider themselves unaffiliated with any particular church denomination.

Demographically, you will likely discover that the majority of those seeking your services will be professional couples in their mid twenties, although you will find yourself asked to serve a fascinating variety of brides and grooms.

Couples today are seeking out Humanistic ceremonies and Celebrants because they offer a hugely personal touch to their day. A Humanist ceremony offers a couple great freedom of expression and a chance to build an occasion that reflects their personality and story. They are finding that they are being given an opportunity to build a wedding ceremony where every word and gesture reflects their lives, their history together, and their dreams.

Officiating a Humanist wedding is a hugely positive and rewarding experience which will leave you with memories you will treasure long after the event.

2.2 - What is a Humanist Wedding?

A Humanist wedding is, above all else, a celebration of love, life, caring, and hope. The primary focus of this type of ceremony is on the couple and does so in a very natural and honest way. There is no need, or desire, to reference supernatural forces or mythological entities. These are considered an unnecessary, and frequently unwanted, distraction from the couple and the important vows they are making.

There are no formal ceremonial traditions in Humanism, and no edicts to Humanist Celebrants which demand particular forms, or structures, within a ceremony. Because of this, each occasion can be, and indeed should be, beautifully unique. A Humanist wedding ceremony can certainly reflect the cultural background of a couple, and their community, but the true mark of a Humanist ceremony is that it is first formed, and created, by the couple. The ceremony is a reflection of their wishes rather than forcing them to obey a set of mandated forms or formulas.

A shared characteristic of the vast majority of Humanist weddings is that they are fun. Although the vows taken are serious and sincere, a wedding is a time for celebration and joy rather than bowed headed solemnity. You may often be asked to include jokes, or touching references, to amuse family and guests, and this is in no way disrespectful. A Humanist wedding is about *joy*. If created and performed with a genuine love and hope, even the more religious among the guests may find themselves moved in a way which many might describe as spiritual. For Humanists, this is the spirit of our natural Humanism at its very best. Positivity is at the core of, and the driving force behind, a truly Humanist wedding.

In summary, a Humanist wedding is:

- Focused on the couple, their love, hopes, and commitment.
- Based on a natural viewpoint of a treasured, finite, earthly life.
- Unconstrained by tradition or dogma.
- Flexible to the wishes of the couple.
- A fun celebration, rather than a somber, reverential, occasion.
- Focused on values of love, compassion, equality, responsibility, and human potential, not on religious tenets.
- The vows spoken are made to each other and not to, or in front of, any supernatural authority.

2.3 - The Role of a Wedding Celebrant

At a Humanist wedding, the role of the Celebrant is to preside and facilitate rather than restrain or dictate. You are there to work with, and for, the couple. Your job is to give them a ceremony which reflects their wishes, hopes, their personalities, individually and together and an event which suits practical factors such as the venue, the number of guests, and time of day.

Many couples come to their Celebrant armed only with the knowledge that they want to marry. They may have booked a venue and other vendors but the actual process of building a ceremony may be somewhat of a mystery to them. The Celebrant's job is to introduce them to the possibilities, the usual elements that others have chosen, and all the options, and additions they might consider. Together, you will build something truly personal and satisfying.

The process will often start with an initial contact with one of the couple, though on occasions this may be a parent or a wedding planner. If you connect, in terms of availability and interest, you will then need to arrange a more extensive consultation.

2.4 - Meeting with the Couple

Ideally, your main consultation will be a meeting with the couple in person. Where this is not possible, for reasons of time and distance, an online video call through a service such as Skype or Google Hangouts can make a highly effective alternative. Failing those options, a teleconference can be sufficient for talking through ceremony plans.

The relationship between the Celebrant and the couple can develop into one of close trust and friendship. I believe the very best ceremonies are created where a human bond and understanding is well established. For this reason, I think it inadvisable to carry out the entire process of creating the ceremony only through e-mail or a third party. For building a Humanist ceremony, there is no substitute for human contact.

If you are able to meet with a couple personally it is wise to choose a venue which gives you the appropriate atmosphere. You may choose to interview the couple in your home or in theirs. However, many prefer to meet at a café or restaurant. It is best to pick a spacious venue with tables sizable enough to spread out your notes and paperwork. Chain coffee shops may seem a good choice but many are often crowded and noisy and have tables barely larger than a dinner plate. It is better to pick a venue which has booths as these are more suited to both comfort and privacy. Additionally, you will often be asked to meet outside normal business hours as many couples have standard day jobs. You should consider whether your meeting venue will remain open and comfortable during those times.

2.5 - The Key Players

Bride. The woman, or the term for the individual presented by an escort at the start of the ceremony.

Groom. The man, or the term for the receiving partner.

Groomsmen. A selection of men chosen by the couple to represent the Groom's support in the ceremony. One is often chosen to be the Best Man, the senior groomsmen, who will often hold the rings prior to their exchange.

Bridesmaids. A selection of women chosen by the couple to represent the Bride's support in the ceremony. One is often chosen to be the Maid of Honor, if unmarried, or Matron of Honor, if married. The M.O.H. will usually stand beside the bride and will often have the task of holding the bride's bouquet during the ceremony.

Escort. An individual chosen to formally escort the bride during the ceremony and often to act as an official representative of her family when handing off the bride to be wed.

Ring Bearer. Usually this is a younger member of either family chosen to be a real or symbolic bearer of the wedding bands into the ceremony. In some cases a pet may be assigned this role.

Flower Girl. Usually a younger female member of a family, asked to walk before the bride carrying and distributing a container of flower petals.

Planner or Coordinator. A trusted professional hired to organize and plan the wedding event.

2.6 - Legal Ceremonies and Commitment Ceremonies

It is important to know the legal status of the ceremony you are planning to perform.

If a couple is already married, and you are being asked to perform a "cosmetic" ceremony, be sure to ask who among their family and friends is aware of this situation. Occasionally, secondary ceremonies are held so as not to offend particular relatives by admitting that a couple was married without them present. More often, it is to fulfill the dream of a "grand" ceremony after a previous, purely legal, event has taken place.

2.7 - Same Sex Weddings

It is wonderful to see that America is moving quickly to embrace same sex equality. There are surprisingly few differences between a same sex and a different sex wedding ceremony. For a Celebrant, the most important difference to understand is one of terminology. Although in this book I have used the words "bride" and "groom" for convenience, these may not be applicable to a same sex marriage occasion.

When working with a same sex couple, it is important to ask how they would like to be addressed during the ceremony. As with all other Humanist ceremonies, the nature and language of the occasion should reflect the nature of the couple's relationship.

In almost all other comparisons to a different sex marriage, a same sex marriage takes place in much the same way, and that is exactly how it should be.

2.8 - The "Cosmetic" Ceremony

Cosmetic ceremonies occur when a couple have already been legally married, but they wish a ceremony to celebrate, or to publically announce, their marriage among family and friends.

A small number of couples will approach you to perform a wedding ceremony despite being legally married on a previous date.

If you can, ask the couple to read, or repeat, the vows they gave in their original ceremony. Where this is not possible, or not desired, they might like to offer a new or updated set of vows to each other in one of the formats described below.

As with each ceremony you perform, the wishes of the couple should be your guide to creating and performing the occasion.

2.9 - Vow Renewals

A great many couples now choose to celebrate a milestone in their marriage by renewing their vows to each other. As a celebration of continuing love, this is something Humanists should applaud.

A renewal of vows is very much like the original wedding ceremony in that it is both formal and orchestrated. There is rarely a procession or recession but rather the request, or "summoning", of the couple to stand before others.

It may often be that one of a couple chooses to surprise the other by presenting them with an opportunity for vow renewal. You should always be aware of the background, and circumstances, of each ceremony you are asked to perform.

If you are asked to write opening or closing remarks, it can be very useful to interview friends and family members beforehand.

The majority of vow renewals take place in settings which are more informal than those of a wedding ceremony.

There are no legal requirements for a renewal of vows. This should not prevent you from treating them with the full dignity you would give every wedding ceremony.

2.10 - Template Ceremonies

Many Celebrants choose to create a portfolio of ceremonies which they then offer to each couple. Each of these may then have the names, and a few other textual aspects, replaced before the ceremony is performed.

You may choose to offer your services this way, but it is not in the spirit of the personalized ceremonies a couple may expect when seeking a Humanist Celebrant.

It can be useful to keep a "standard" ceremony printed for occasions when you may be contacted to perform an "elopement" or court house wedding. On such occasions you may decide to charge less than your usual fee for officiating.

It is important always to remember that we are serving individuals, and a community, and be reflexive to, and understanding of, their needs and ability to compensate us for our work.

2.11 - Relationship Biographies

If we want to be able to work with a couple to build a ceremony which reflects their history, personality, and hopes, we have to know something of their lives. It is obviously impractical to become intimate friends with every couple for whom we officiate. We therefore need a shortcut to understanding their story.

One method is to ask the couple to each produce a "relationship biography". This details their own recollections and perspectives of their romance from its very beginning to the present. It is best to ask a couple to produce these separately and in whichever style and format feels most comfortable. Some individuals may produce just a few bullet points, but more often the "flood gates" of storytelling will open, and you will receive heartfelt, and deeply moving, tales of some length. The longest narrative I have personally received was over six thousand words long. This process seems to be truly enjoyable for most couples as a chance to relive the highlights of their courtship.

These biographies give us two important types of information. Firstly, they give us insights into the styles and personalities of the couple. Secondly, they highlight the important themes and events which have shaped their time together. If a specific story or theme appears in both texts we know it is of particular importance. This provides a wonderful starting point for the ceremony, and particularly in creating parts such as the opening address and closing statement.

2.12 - Core Elements of a Wedding Ceremony

What then are the "core" or "standard" parts of a Humanist wedding ceremony? Although it has been strongly emphasized that each occasion should be made unique, there are elements which appear at the core of almost every modern Western wedding.

2.12a - Processional

At its simplest, the processional is the method of bringing all the members of the wedding party to their starting positions for the ceremony. Most weddings begin with a formal entry for those involved.

There is no prescribed order for entry or who must be included. For smaller weddings it can be as few as only the groom, bride, and her escort. A common larger order of entry might be:

- Officiant
- Parents of the Groom
- Mother of the Bride plus her Escort
- Groom
- Groomsmen
- Ring Bearer
- Bridesmaids
- Flower Girl
- Bride plus Escort

Some couples may like to include grandparents in the formal procession, while others may like to have the groom enter at the very beginning to act as a "greeter" for the wedding party. It is important to listen to the wishes of the couple and to present them with the benefits of every option they may wish to consider.

There are other points you may wish to note:

1. It is usual, but not essential, that the Groom and Groomsmen stand to THEIR right of the aisle as they approach. This means they would stand on YOUR left.

2. It is usual for the Celebrant to ask the guests to rise at the point in the processional where the bride begins her entrance and then to ask them to be seated once she is in position and has been presented by her escort if that element is included.

2.12b - The "Presentation of the Bride" or "Giving Away"

A presentation of the bride, commonly called the "giving away", can occur once the bride and escort have arrived to stand before the Celebrant and the groom. This is certainly not required for every ceremony but can nicely represent love, and commitment, transferring across the generations of each family.

There are several general options for this part of the ceremony.

1. The escort, perhaps a father, mother, or brother, can simply hug the bride and then hug or shake the hand of the Groom before the escort is then seated.

2. Where a "question" is requested to be given by the Celebrant, it can be appropriate to use simple, modern language. An example might be, "Who presents this woman to be married?"

3. The couple may request a second parent, or grandparent, to step forward to join the escort before any formal question is given.

4. It is possible to expand the giving away by officially asking the parents or families of both Bride and Groom for their approval, or "blessing", of the wedding. This can be done in turn or in unison.

Here the term "blessing" is a secular one, as you are asking for the approval of human beings rather than requesting it of any supernatural entity.

5. If a couple wishes to take the process of giving away to its ultimate extreme you could ask the blessing, or approval, of all those present. I have often advised against this, as it can cause a little confusion or worse give cause for a "comedian" among the guests to call out something "amusing". For this reason, asking if anybody formally objects to the wedding, often referred to as "speak now or forever hold your peace", has fallen greatly out of fashion and should usually be discouraged.

2.12c - Opening Words

Once all are the participants are in position and the guests are seated, it is time to begin the ceremony proper. The opening words, spoken by the Celebrant, welcome everyone and explain how and why the couple has chosen to stand before everyone on this day. As well as giving the essence of their story, you may wish to cover the importance of vows, commitment, and the marking of important moments publicly within our community.

It is here that the relationship biographies, as described above, can gain true importance. These can be invaluable in giving a personal and unique flavor to the content of your words.

It is useful to ask the couple if there are any people or events they particularly wish referenced in the words you speak during the ceremony. These can include individuals such as grandparents, if they had a strong influence on their relationship, or a beloved pet, if it played a significant part in their bonding as a couple.

It is equally important to ensure you do not mention any aspect of their life which they would rather was left out. Such items might include previous romantic relationships.

Some couples may wish you to make reference to children they each bring to their family or those they have already parented together. Alternatively, a couple may wish to exclude all references to children, where they have no intent in having any offspring.

The more you learn and understand of a couple, the easier it will be to see what would work best in any opening address. You should be careful to ask exactly which name each chooses to be referred to during the ceremony. Although a person is known by one name informally in public, they may wish to be addressed more formally for the purpose of the ceremony. For example, a woman known as Liz to many on a daily basis may wish to be addressed as Elizabeth during her wedding.

For a Celebrant who is not a keen writer, there a great many sample openings available online, or in books, which could be used. By altering just a few words and phrases, these could be adapted to give some excellent personalization to any address.

I strongly recommend developing your writing skills, to give these a segments a strong and clear style.

You should carefully read through each passage you intend to speak at the ceremony, and ideally practice these out loud to a trusted friend, or a family member, to gain important, objective, feedback on what you have created and assembled.

An ideal length for an opening address may be between 200 and 300 words. It is important not to bore an assembled group but also not to have them feel that you are rushing the proceedings.

2.12d - Vows

Vows are the cornerstone of any marriage ceremony. They are the opportunity for each to look into the other's eyes and make the most important pledge of their relationship. In a Humanist wedding ceremony, these vows are *not* made in front of, or under the patriarchal eye of, a deity. They are given from one human heart and life to another. They are secured not by fear of damnation but by love, kindness, and honesty.

In the broadest terms, vows come in three general, but not exclusive, types:

Recited, or Self-Written Words.

Some couples choose to write their own vows to be read to each other on the day. In many cases, such vows are kept secret from their partner until the moment they are given. Where couples express a wish to include this type of vow, you may want to offer the following advice:

1. Decide whether to keep your vows secret until the wedding day.

It can be powerful and emotional for partners to hear the others vows and promises for the very first time on the wedding day. Many couples choose to keep their most personal words secret until the big moment. Of course, there is no obligation to do so. Some couples find it romantic to work on their vows together, especially if these are to be repeated lines rather than a statement of promises to be read aloud. This is your wedding to build in your way.

2. Decide on the style and tone of your vows.

It is very important that you have a balance in the vows you both create not only in length but also in style. If one of you reads several paragraphs, and the other just a few lines, it can make the latter seem a little stingy. Just as important, is deciding on a tone which matches. If only one of you gives beautiful lyrical verses, while the other makes jokes about the pets or the Netflix queue, it may make one or both of you a little uncomfortable on the day. Perhaps the most important factor is that your vows reflect your personalities both individually and as a couple. It will feel most beautiful, personal, and sincere if you use a style and voice that resonates from the real you. Vows are a statement from the heart. There is no right or wrong, only honesty, commitment, and love.

3. Decide how long your vows will be.

It is important that your vows cover all the important things you want to say to your partner, but the most powerful vows are tightly written and of a length which fits with the rest of the ceremony. For a written statement of promises, a good length is usually between 150 and 200 words. Your vows should not normally last more than two minutes. If you find you are writing more, why not see if you are repeating ideas or if your statements might sound better written more concisely.

4. Start by putting your ideas on paper.

Begin preparing your vows by making notes. Why not write out a list of twelve key things you want to say: six which tell your partner how you feel, and six which tell them of your hopes for your future together. Once you have listed these thoughts, consider how you might state each in the form of a promise. Once you have these, decide on the order you wish to say them. It is nice to state first why you love your partner, and how you promise to always love them, followed by all the things you hope to do and share in the years to come and how you pledge to help make these happen. Again, the most important thing is that your vows sound as though they come from your heart and that they truly speak with your own voice. The more personal your vows sound, the more powerful, and moving, they will be.

5. Watch for some possible pitfalls.

As you write and edit your vows, guard against clichés. It is much nicer to say things in your own way rather than in the words of others. Watch out for references which may be obscure or cryptic. Although you are writing for each other, it is nice for the guests to understand everything you say and not feel locked out from any private joke or unexplained reference. You should also take care that you are not saying anything which may embarrass one or both of you. Even in front of your friends and family, it can be best to be discrete about the most private things you share. If you find you have more to say, of a private and personal nature, why not agree to also exchange letters with your partner on your wedding day saying even more in the very special way you talk to each other when you are alone.

6. Try practicing your vows out loud.

The best way to test how your vows will sound on the day is to read them aloud. As you do this, you will quickly notice any lines which sound awkward, any words which you may have difficulty pronouncing, and anywhere the flow feels a little broken or confused. Remember, you are writing to be spoken, and so your sentences should be a little shorter and simpler than if written to be read silently.

7. Have your Celebrant or friend give a second opinion.

Once you have a draft of the vows you feel happy with, it is an excellent idea to get a fresh opinion. This can be from either a friend, who can give you an excellent idea of how your guests will hear you and understand you, or from your Celebrant, who has plenty of experience as to what sounds best on the day. As you stand in front of your partner, you will be saying your vows in front of others, perhaps many guests, friends, and family. Why not have trial runs with somebody you trust and are comfortable speaking in front of.

8. Create a beautiful copy of your vows for your wedding day.

You should *not* try to memorize anything you are to say during your wedding ceremony. You will therefore need a physical copy of your vows to read on the day. These look best printed on a nice piece of card, perhaps colored to match the colors you have chosen for your day. To make it as easy as possible to read, be sure to print in a large font. It is also a good idea to break the printed lines up into phrases rather than leave as full paragraphs. Whatever makes your vows easier to read will be hugely helpful as you stand, nervously, during the big moment.

9. Keep a copy of your vows to remind you of the day.

If you have put a lot of thought into your vows, and truly spoken of your heart and hopes, it is nice to keep these thoughts with you as you travel together down the married years to come. Why not keep a copy of your words for your scrapbook or somewhere else you can view from time to time, and so have something always there to remind you, especially during any dark times, of why you walked the aisle and why you chose to share your life with the person you love.

Where couples decide on writing their own vows in this manner, it is important that the Celebrant review each text before the day. This will ensure that they balance each other and have good readability. It is also a good practice for the Celebrant to provide the printed cards to be read from on the day. You should ensure that these are in a large font and written in a way easy to scan with the eye. Under no circumstances should you encourage a couple to attempt to memorize their vows for the ceremony.

Repeated Lines

In this case the Celebrant feeds each partner, in turn, a set of lines, promises, or phrases which they then repeat. Usually these are written by the Celebrant, but occasionally the couple may decide to write these lines themselves.

It is a good idea to ask the couple to list the things they wish to promise the other before you create such a text.

An example of a modern set of repeated lines, which I have used on several occasions, is:

I take you to be my best friend,
My lifelong partner and my love.
I vow to help you love life.
I promise I will always try my best
To have the patience, and understanding, that love demands.
I vow to be open with you.
I promise to encourage you
And truly appreciate you
And the happiness you bring me every day.
I promise to love you through good times and bad.
I will forever be there to laugh with you,
To lift you up when you are down,
And to love you unconditionally
Through all of our adventures in life together.

The "Putting of the Question"

With this option, the Celebrant poses a set of formal questions, regarding the obligations of love and marriage, to which the expected answer is "I Do".

For couples embarrassed by speaking in public, this can be a popular option.

An example of a modern question might be:

Do you take [Bride or Groom],
To love with all your heart,
To live together and laugh together,
To work by your side,
To seek the best in them,
And give the best of yourself,
To always comfort and understand them,
To grow together all your days,
as long as you both shall live?

Many couples choose a combination of the above options. They may choose to make a personal statement, or to repeat some given lines, followed by the putting of the question.

The Celebrant's job is to help each couple discover, and craft, the option which will best fit their styles and personalities.

2.12e - Exchange of Rings

Not all couples choose to exchange rings. For those who do, this can be one of the simplest parts of the ceremony for you to create. The greatest difficulty may be to decide on which member of the wedding party will bear the rings on the day, before they are offered, and to instruct that person in their duties.

A note on Ring Bearers. Many couples choose a younger member of the family to bear the rings during the processional. For boys or girls under the age of five, it can be a sensible precaution to make them a "symbolic" ring bearer. In such a case, the child would carry a box or cushion with them but not the valuable rings themselves which would be held by another member of the wedding party such as a groomsman. On rare occasions, a couple may wish a pet to act as a ring bearer. In such a case, it is always better that their beloved animal is not, in reality, entrusted with the jewelry.

The exchange of rings is usually conducted with the groom first placing the ring on the bride's third finger of her left hand. While doing so, he may simultaneously repeat a few symbolic lines. The bride then repeats the exchange in a similar manner.

A note on Engagement Rings. It is traditional that the wedding ring is placed "closest to the heart" by which is meant closest to the knuckle. In practice, this means that any engagement ring should be held elsewhere until the wedding ring is in place. Many brides choose to hold their engagement ring on the right hand, and then slip it over the wedding ring once that has been given. Some brides choose to leave the engagement ring off completely for the ceremony. Another option is to have a jeweler fix both rings together as one before the ceremony and so for all time. Some ring combinations are designed especially for that option.

As with all traditions, in a Humanist ceremony there is no requirement for any rules, or formats, to be followed. The couple should be made aware of all their options, and choose which they feel is most appropriate.

2.12f - Closing Words

The closing words a Celebrant speaks at the end of the ceremony provide a counterpoint to those given in the opening. Whereas the opening words might address the story and events which brought the couple together, and so led to the wedding day, the closing words might address the obligations, hopes, and wishes all those in attendance have for the years to come.

2.12g - Pronouncements and Presentation

It is usual, at the close of the ceremony, for the Celebrant to formally pronounce a couple married and present them to those gathered.

For the pronouncement, it is usual, and traditional, to speak something akin to "By the power vested in my by..." Although Humanist ceremonies often break with tradition, this is often expected by couples, family, and guests.

The question, for any Humanist Celebrant, is which authority you choose to name. Some Celebrants may choose to name their body of ordination such as "by the Society of Celebrations". Far more common is to name the state, or principality, in which you are performing the ceremony. This makes greater sense, as it is those bodies which create the rules for who may solemnize a marriage, and also because they are spiritually "neutral" and can thus meet the expectations of all those in attendance without provoking controversy.

For the words of presentation, if giving the couple a title, there are many options the bride and groom might like to choose. Most couples will not have considered this aspect, and there are many choices:

Mr. and Mrs. John Smith
Mr. John and Mrs. Jane Smith
Mr. and Mrs. Smith
Jane and John
John and Jane
Husband and Wife
The Smiths
etc.

The version they choose should be the one which suits them best and by which they feel they would be most comfortable being known. When presented with the above options, most couples will very quickly know which they prefer.

As a final symbolic element, most couples choose to close their ceremony with a kiss. I have always found it a little concerning when a couple chooses not to do this. For the benefit of the photographer, it is advisable they hold the kiss for at least six seconds.

Tip: When the couple move to give their final kiss, it is wise to take a step to the side and thus avoid "photo bombing" an important moment in their wedding album. I would suggest that, if you are a male Celebrant you step back and to the groom's side, and if a female Celebrant you step back and to the side of the bride's group.

2.12h - Recessional

As a counterpoint to the processional, the recessional is the way in which the wedding party makes their formal departure, at the conclusion of the ceremony.

Aside from the exit of the bride and groom together, the recessional is often, in great part, a reverse of the processional order.

Tip: When you are planning the processional and recessional, you may wish to have the groomsmen and bridesmaids enter separately at the beginning of the ceremony, and depart in pairs at its end. Not only does this offer the photographer a greater variety of shots, but it also gives further symbolism to the union of the couple.

For the recessional, you will often find it is your role to give cues to the participants as to when to begin their exit walk. In doing so, you should consider the time needed for a photographer to obtain all the pictures they require as well as the distance each party must walk to their destination. It is important not to rush the proceedings. Members of the wedding party are sure to be eager to exit, and your role at such times is to keep the pace steady.

As you will likely be the last to recess, you may well find it useful, or required, that you say parting words to the guests. You may wish to thank them for attending, but more importantly you may wish to instruct them how to exit and where to go for the next part of the day. Often the guests are required to attend a cocktail hour while the bridal party takes photographs or the couple changes clothing. Some instructions from you at this time can be very useful.

You may wish to exit in a different manner to the bridal party. Having presided, some Celebrants choose to exit to the side rather than proceed down the aisle. Consult with the couple, or ideally the venue coordinator, to discover which might be the most appropriate option.

2.13 - The "Through Line" of the Ceremony

You will notice two patterns within the structure of most wedding ceremonies. Firstly, the earlier parts of the ceremony are most usually associated with the events, and emotions, which brought the couple to the day. The later elements more usually reflect the dreams, hopes, and obligations for the future. Secondly, you will notice that the elements of the ceremony bring the couple progressively physically closer. The bride approaches and is presented. After this they each face the other for their vows. They touch during the exchange of rings. Finally, they come together for the marriage kiss. An understanding of these patterns is a great advantage in creating a clean, and coherently structured, ceremony.

2.14 - Ceremonial Music

Music is often an important part of a marriage ceremony. The majority of ceremonies, whether employing live music or a DJ, utilize four key musical elements:

1. A medley, or "prelude", for the seating of the guests.

2. A chosen theme for the entrance of the main wedding party.

3. A specific theme for the entrance of the Bride and Escort.

4. An upbeat theme for the Recessional.

You may often find it is your job to provide a subtle cue for the musician or DJ to start, and stop, tunes and transition between musical elements. At some venues, the musician may not be able to see the wedding party enter and so may rely on you to indicate when this is happening. In physical terms, a good cue is a clear and dignified nod.

It is wise to converse briefly with musicians before the ceremony to establish all the required cues are in place and known to all.

Musical Interludes during the Ceremony

Many couples may have in mind a pause during the ceremony for the playing of a particular song. Although the wishes of the couple are paramount in the planning process, it is also the job of the Celebrant to advise on such decisions. It is a sad but unavoidable truth that musical "interludes" during a wedding ceremony are almost always an obstruction to the proceedings. Placing a song between spoken elements can create a disruptive hiatus during which the majority of the guests can become bored. They spend these times only in eagerly awaiting its conclusion.

2.15 - Photography

Photography is an important element of many weddings. Many couples will have hired a professional photographer, or a photographic team, to cover their day. As a Celebrant, it is advisable to liaise briefly with the photographer to ensure they know the rules, and format, of the ceremony. It will be very useful to the photographer to know where participants will stand and what the verbal cues will be for important moments such as the final kiss.

If you have decided on adding a unity element to your ceremony, it will be useful for the photographer to know where, how, and when this will happen, and so ensure they are in the correct position.

If you choose, or are asked, to give a brief welcome to the guests before the processional, you may wish to say a few words about cell phones. Many couples, and photographers, strongly prefer guests *not* take photographs during the course of the ceremony. There are several reasons for this. Firstly, the presence of hands raised holding cell phones can hurt the look of an official photograph. Secondly, if a photographer gets into position to take an important picture and a guest moves out of place to take their own it can spoil a moment of opportunity for the professional. Such a moment can never be repeated. Many twenty first century couples are also unhappy with guest photographers, as they have no wish for candid shots to be posted on social networks before they have been approved.

Tip: Avoid bright colors in your garb, but most especially red. In photographs, red items and clothing are most arresting to the eye. A bright and eye-catching Celebrant could distract unnecessarily from the most important figures of the day. You should remember that this is always the bride and groom.

2.16 - Additional Ceremonial Elements

Although the above provides a basic structure for most wedding ceremonies, there are many wonderful additions which can be made to the occasion. These can give a unique and memorable experience to the wedding party and their guests. Below are some additions you might consider.

2.17 - Readings

There is a long tradition of having important, or significant, texts or passages read during a wedding ceremony. One great beauty of Humanist ceremonies is that these readings may be from any source relevant, resonant, or meaningful to the couple. You do not, by any means, need to confine readings to religious texts or scripture. Readings can include poems, song lyrics, theatrical speeches, or letters. They can include any text from sources as diverse as Dante and Winnie the Pooh.

The most important factor with any reading is that the meaning and style resonate with the story and relationship of the bride and groom. In some cases, the bride and groom may wish to "gift" a reading to each other. These can be gifts of great romance and beautiful significance.

Where a couple is acquainted with keen speakers, or theatrical friends, asking those people to present a reading can be a marvelous way of involving them in the wedding day. Often, however, the Celebrant is asked to give the reading as an integrated part of their statements.

If, as a Celebrant, you are asked to read from another source, you should try to adjust your tone slightly from that used in other parts of the proceedings. In all you say, it is important to have a varied tone and emphasis rather than speak in a staccato or flat manner which would dull the emotion of your words.

Tip: Although friends and family readers may bring their own printed sheet to read from, too often this is a folded sheet of printer paper with printing in a small font. This can appear as though the reader is improperly prepared and can look very unattractive. If the reader has to strain to see their words, or prevent their sheet from flapping in the breeze, they will have trouble concentrating on their performance. It is better to obtain a piece of quality card stock, and print the text in a large, clear font.

Keep all of the text for a reading to a single side, and lay out the lines, phrase by phrase, as they should be spoken. This will allow a reader to give their very best rendition of the chosen piece.

Some Suggested Readings

Below is a selection of readings which the author has found to work well in practice. In order to save space, and for obvious copyright reasons, the full texts are not reproduced here. All of these suggestions can be found, freely available, online. This list is by no means definitive. Encourage every couple to be creative, and also to pick readings which truly reflect their style, personalities, and story.

1. *"I Fell In Love With Her Courage" by F. Scott Fitzgerald*

2. *"The Awakened Heart" by Gerald May*

3. *"The Laws of Wellness" by Greg Anderson*

4. "Ever After" by C.S. Lewis

5. "Let Love Be Stronger Than Your Anger" by Unknown

6. "A Small Poem Of Happiness" by Neil Gaiman

7. "Soul Mates" by Lang Leav

8. "The Road Not Taken" by Robert Frost

9. "To Love is Not to Possess" by James Kavanaugh

10. Traditional Apache Marriage Blessing

11. "Blessing For A Marriage" by James Dillet Freeman

12. "How Do I Love Thee" by Elizabeth Barrett Browning

13. First Corinthians, Chapter 13 [Biblical verse that does not invoke the supernatural]

14. "Union From The Beginning To End" by Robert Fulghum

15. "The Point of Marriage" by Rene Maria Rilke

16. "Yes, I'll Marry You" by Pam Ayres

17. "The Art Of Marriage" by Wilford A. Peterson

18. "Now We Are Six" by A. A. Milne

19. "To Love is Not to Possess" by James Kavanaugh

20. "Marriage Joins Two People In The Circle Of Its Love" By Edmund O'Neill

21. "Never Marry But For Love" by William Penn

22. "The Confirmation" By Edwin Muir

23. "He Never Leaves The Seat Up" by Unknown

24. "Oh the Places You'll Go" by Dr Seuss

25. "Corelli's Mandolin" by Louis De Bernieres

26. Hindu Marriage Poem

27. "Falling in love is like owning a dog" Taylor Mali

28. "A Natural History of Love" by Diane Ackerman

29. "Gift From The Sea" by Anne Morrow Lindbergh

30. "The Key to Love" by Anon, 1st century China

31. "Sooner or Later" by Unknown

32. "The Passionate Shepherd to His Love" by Christopher Marlowe

33. "The Irrational Season" by Madeleine L'Engle

34. "A Lovely Love Story" by Edward Monkton

35. "A Love Knot"

36. "I'll Be There For You" By Louise Cuddon

37. "I Like You" by Sandol Stoddard Warburg

38. "I Rely On You" by Hovis Presley

39. "I Wanna Be Yours" By John Cooper-Clarke

40. "Recipe for Love" by Unknown

41. "The Owl and the Pussycat" by Edward Lear

42. "The House at Pooh Corner" by A.A Milne

43. "Untitled" by Bee Rawlinson

44. "Weddings" by Unknown

45. "Blessing for a Marriage" by James Dillet Freeman

46. "The Art of Marriage" by Wilferd Arlan Peterson

47. "Love" by Roy Croft

48. "The Awakened Heart" by Gerald May

49. "Dao de Jing" by Laozi

50. "Why Marriage?" by Mari Nichols-Haining

2.18 - Unity Ceremonies

A Unity Ceremony can make an impressive addition to any wedding, and these can bring something different to simply listening to an officiant speak. What follows is a list of some of the ideas a couple might use to make their moment even more special.

There is no strict rule as to where unity rituals should take place in the ceremony, but typically one is placed directly after the exchange of vows and rings.

2.18a - Unity Candle

Although the Unity Candle has somewhat gained a reputation as the "classic" unity ceremony, it is actually a relatively new tradition. It has, however, declined in popularity in recent times, as many venues have fire regulations prohibiting open flames. For outdoor ceremonies it is often impractical.

The unity candle ceremony uses two taper candles with a large pillar candle in the center. At the beginning of the wedding ceremony representatives from each family, usually the mothers of the bride and groom, light the two taper candles. Later in the ceremony, usually after the vows, the bride and groom use the two taper candles to light the large pillar candle in unison.

Often, a unity candle is decorated with the wedding invitation, an inscription, a picture of the couple, or other ornamentation. The candles are almost always white. The lighting ceremony may be accompanied by special music. The couple may choose to save the unity candle and then to relight it on their wedding anniversaries.

2.18b - Sand Ceremony

Especially in coastal areas, sand ceremonies have become increasingly popular in recent years.

Three Vessels

Typically, each person has different colored sand and takes turns pouring it into one clear vessel forming a layered effect. Complete sets for these are available widely online and in many craft shops. The receiving vessel can make a very nice ornamental keepsake.

Family Sand Ceremony

Although most sand ceremonies involve only the bride and groom, it can be nice to involve other family members, especially where one, or both, of the couple bring children with them to the marriage. These ceremonies can be a beautiful way to make children feel included by giving them their own special color of sand which they then add to the blend.

Beach Sand Ceremonies

On a beach, where sand is of course plentiful, there are other possible variations. Each of the couple might scoop sand from the ground beneath the others feet, and this could then be mingled in a bowl or simply allowed to pour through their partners upturned hands.

Hourglass Variation

In this variation the sands are poured into an hourglass which is then sealed, kept, and turned once a year on the anniversary of their wedding.

Hometown Earth Ceremony

For a special celebration of the mingling of two histories, it may be possible to obtain samples of earth from each partner's hometown and mix these together instead of sand.

2.18c - Flower Ceremony

A wedding flower ceremony can be symbolic in many ways. Simply by virtue of having roots, and being inclined to growth, plants make excellent metaphors for marriage, where many couples wish to honor their families of origin yet look towards their future together. Blossoms evoke images of beauty, joy, potential, and fertility. This can also be a great opportunity to involve parents or children in the ceremony. The color and type of flower can be chosen to represent or amplify many themes relevant to weddings and marriage.

Lei / Garland Ceremony

The Lei exchange ceremony has its roots in Hawaiian culture, while the giving of garlands has a strong tradition in India. In a modern, secular, ceremony, the garlands can be exchanged at any time from the start to the close of the ceremony. Additionally, they can be presented to, or by, parents or children. The choice of colors can be symbolic or simply designed to blend in with those used across the day in general.

2.18d - Knot Ceremonies

The ceremonial tying of knots is another addition which has become very popular in recent years, and this can be performed in a variety of ways. Most usually, the marriage knot is secured at the end of the ceremony to symbolize the couple's final pledge to bind their lives together.

Handfasting

There are many ways to perform a handfasting ceremony. The number of cords used can vary, as can the color, and these can be used to symbolize any number of things. In a handfasting, the cords are often draped rather than tied. Typically, a couple will take turns draping the cords while repeating vows or while listening to statements given by the Celebrant. As you can see, this is an incredibly versatile addition to any wedding.

Fisherman's Knot

A Fisherman's Knot is a wonderful, and highly symbolic, adaptation of the traditional knot tying ceremony. It gives the couple something both beautiful and fascinating to share in. For those unfamiliar with this knot there are helpful videos available online. Perhaps more than any other type of knot ritual, this demands that the couple practice the ceremony beforehand, but that can be a fun way to pass an evening!

Tying of the Braid

Once again, tying a braid represents the joining of lives. Some may interpret the use of three cords as having the religious symbolism of a "holy trinity". However, this ritual could be a beautiful Humanistic addition, where one or more children are also coming together as a new family. The colors of the cords used could be symbolic or chosen to blend in with the themes of the day. Such a finished braid could then be hung in the home as a keepsake for many years to come.

2.18e - Wine Ceremony

Typically, a table is set out with a bottle of wine, or a decanted carafe, chosen to suit the couple. Sometimes, the Celebrant will pour the wine for the couple, as often they have the steadiest hand, but sometimes the couple will pour a glass for each other and then exchange these between themselves.

On occasion, the couple may want to pour two different wines into one goblet for them both to drink from. In this case, it is important to choose wines which will blend well and please the palate.

Wine and Chocolate Ceremony

One variation of the wine ceremony also adds chocolate, as this is something the couple may have a passion to share. The idea is to represent both the sour and the sweet moments that we encounter in life and to show that whichever of these may come, from this point forward, they will always be faced and conquered side by side.

2.18f - Time Capsule

The Time Capsule is a beautiful idea which has gained increasing popularity in recent years. The couple provides letters to each other along perhaps with a bottle of something special and perhaps a copy of their vows. These are placed inside a ceremonial container and the couple then seals it publicly. The notion is that, at a later date perhaps in a few years or maybe at a time of crisis, the box is opened and they can both relive the memories, and emotions, of the wedding day once again.

2.18g - Water Ceremony

Much like a liquid version of the sand ceremony, the idea is that waters, usually of two different colors, are mingled together to create a new mixture, much as the blending of two loves will create something new.

Hand Wetting

A different variation of this water ceremony concept is for each of the couple to sprinkle water from a bowl over the other's hands. This represents the gift of a clean start to life as well as trust and support. In some cases the sprinkling may be performed by parents or other family members.

2.18h - Bread Breaking Ceremony

The idea of breaking bread stems from an eastern European tradition where each of the couple takes a bite, or a "chunk", from a loaf, and the one who manages the biggest becomes the "leader" of the household. Of course, you don't need the competition element. Bread, broken and offered, can be symbolic of many things from the joining of two families, particularly if the mothers baked the bread, to the founding of a new home.

2.18i - Coin Ceremony

The custom of the giving of wedding coins originated in Spain. Thirteen gold coins, or "arras", are given by the bridegroom to the bride signifying his willingness to support her. Often presented in ornate boxes, or gift trays, this represents the bride's dowry and holds good wishes for prosperity.

Of course, coins or tokens can be exchanged either way or brought together collectively. That would symbolize the joining of two incomes into one.

2.18j - Broom Jumping

Jumping the broom is a time-honored wedding tradition that has African American roots. The bride and groom jump over a broom at a key point during the ceremony often to begin the recessional. This act symbolizes a new beginning and a sweeping away of the past. It can also signify the joining of two families or offer a respectful nod to the ancestors of the couple. Most often taking place at the end of the wedding, the couple can jump the broom together, or sometimes separately, after the officiant explains its meaning. The broom itself can be beautifully ornamental and afterwards kept as a keepsake of the day.

2.18k - Oathing Stone

During the reading of the Bride and Groom's wedding vows they may hold an Oathing Stone in their hands. It is believed that holding the stone during the reading of the vows casts those words into the stone. In a more modern version, the Oathing Stone can be engraved with the couple's initials and date of their wedding. The source of an Oathing Stone, what minerals it contains, its color, or other characteristics are less important than what is said over the stone. After the wedding, the stone can be kept as an ornament or keepsake.

2.18l - Truce Bell

In this ritual the couple is presented with a bell during the ceremony, which they can give a symbolic ringing. The idea is that they will take this with them into marred life, and should an argument occur one partner can ring the bell to call for a truce and reconciliation. Other objects can be used instead of a bell. The overriding concept is that it should be used to recall the wonderful feelings they shared that day and use these to lighten any difficult moments or situations to come.

2.18m - Circling Ceremony

Although they have their roots mostly in Jewish traditions, circling ceremonies have a huge variety and can symbolize many things. Circling each other can symbolize protection or creating a new family unit. It has become very common in this ritual for each of the couple to circle the other three times. This can be accompanied by words of explanation, spoken by the Celebrant, or vows or oaths spoken by the bride and groom in turn. Another variation is where the couple asks each other questions and give appropriate responses as they circle the other.

2.18n - The Seven Steps Ceremony

From Hindu tradition, this ceremony involves the bride and groom taking seven steps in a circle often around a fire or other symbolic object. Each step symbolizes a hope for the future. A modern version of the words which accompany the seven steps might read:

1. May this couple be blessed with an abundance of resources and comforts and be helpful to one another in all ways.

2. May this couple be strong and complement one another.

3. May this couple be blessed with prosperity and riches on all levels.

4. May this couple be eternally happy.

5. May this couple be blessed with a happy family life.

6. May this couple live in perfect harmony, and be true to their personal values and joint promises.

7. May this couple always be the best of friends.

2.18o - Salt Ceremony

In some ways the salt ceremony ritual is very like the sand ceremony. Each of the couple brings a container of salt and pours a few grains into that of the other or a larger container. The idea is that the couple is joined until the day one is able to separate their own grains from those of the other. This is, of course, something which is virtually impossible.

Indian Salt Ceremony

Indian weddings often include a Salt Ceremony, where the bride passes a handful of salt to her groom without spilling any. He then passes it back to her, and this exchange is repeated three times. This symbolizes many ideas such as trust and sharing.

2.18p - Tree Planting Ceremony

The unity tree planting ceremony can be used to symbolize the joining together of two individuals or the joining of two families. This is particularly meaningful to couples who feel a special bonding with nature. You might start by setting up a separate table in the ceremony area. On this table, you would place a potted tree or sapling, perhaps of a species with special meaning or taken from a special place. You would also have two small containers of dirt, two gardening trowels, as well as a small watering can placed on the table. If you choose to have the ceremony symbolize the joining together of both families then, upon the entrance of the mothers, each goes to the table and scoops into the container a small amount of dirt. After the ceremony, the couple then plants the tree at their home, or another special location, to symbolize the putting down of roots, longevity, and the strength of their marriage.

2.18q - Unity Painting

A blank canvas strongly represents a new beginning. During this ritual, the couple might pour, or daub, different colors on the canvas symbolically mingling concepts or appropriate ideas. This is a particularly fun ceremony for couples with an artistic inclination. Bear in mind that this can be a messy ceremony to perform and is thus best attempted outdoors. After the wedding, the resultant picture makes a nice artistic keepsake.

2.18r - Tile Breaking Ceremony

The tile breaking originates in Korea but is similar to the Jewish glass breaking of "Mazel Tov". For those unaware, that is the Jewish tradition of the groom breaking a wrapped glass at the end of a ceremony to seal the proceedings. The concept, inherent in both ceremonies, is that what is broken can never be unbroken, and thus the vows which have been made can never be unspoken. With the tile breaking it is important to choose a weak substance, such as terracotta, and make sure it is securely wrapped. In Korean tradition the woman breaks the tile, rather than the man as is the case in Jewish tradition. The tile is often wrapped in a red cloth which symbolizes good luck in many parts of the world.

2.18s - Unity Volcano!

You don't have to be a nerd to enjoy watching the volcano at a science fair. With this ritual, the couple can bring a little science into their wedding. For those unfamiliar with this concept, there are a great many terrific videos and instructions available online.

2.19 - Children and Wedding Ceremonies

Children as participants

Many couples, particularly those who already have children they are bringing to the new family unit, are eager to include their young ones in the ceremony. This can make for some of the most heartwarming, and photogenic, moments of the day. It is important to be aware of the limitations inherent in children of a younger age. Below five years of age, or thereabouts, children can find a role in the ceremony confusing or perhaps even frightening.

Where a very young child is given a role in the procession, there are a few precautions which can help ensure success. If it is possible for a young child to walk with an older sibling or a family member, rather than alone, this can help guide them in their role. Where a young child must walk or perform a task alone it is wise to have an appointed "child wrangler" sat with easy access to where the child will be walking or standing. Such an adult should have one task; knowing that they are appointed to act if the child becomes confused or distressed. Parents and grandparents make the best candidates in these situations.

Children as guests

Very young children can sometimes present more challenges as guests than as participants. Wedding venues and ceremonies can be unsettling and uncomfortable for children under three years of age. They are not yet old enough to understand the significance or etiquette involved in what is taking place around them. Almost all Celebrants have seen ceremonies disrupted, and on occasion spoiled, by the screams and shouts of a young child. Where children are planned to attend it is wise to ask that they be seated with a parent at the rear of the wedding guests and that the parent should be politely instructed to remove the child to a different location should he or she become in any way disruptive. Children are wonderful, but their presence should never impede the experience of the couple in any way.

There is an increasing trend among couples towards "adult only weddings" at which children are specifically prohibited. A wedding day can be an emotional time, often involving adult intoxication and expression, and in those cases may be an inappropriate occasion for children.

2.20 - The Wedding Rehearsal

Deciding whether to hold a rehearsal can be a complicated decision. There is no doubt that everyone begins the actual ceremony with greater confidence when a rehearsal has been held. Sometimes a couple will choose to hold their rehearsal without the presence of the Celebrant, but if one is held I recommend you try to attend. You may often be asked to direct and orchestrate the rehearsal event. It is important to know what should be accomplished. I will begin here by looking at what makes up a wedding rehearsal and then examine the factors which determine how critical a rehearsal is for each planned wedding ceremony.

A wedding rehearsal is about "Who, What, Where, and When".

- Who has a job to do?
- What is that job?
- Where do they do it?
- When do they do it?

A "job" can be as simple as walking from point A to point B. In fact, during a wedding those are some of the most common jobs of all. Everyone from the bride and groom down to the youngest flower girl, if one is appointed, needs to know what is expected of them, where they are expected to walk or stand, and how they get their cue to begin.

In many ways, a wedding rehearsal is like a rehearsal for a piece of theater. Each cast member needs to know when to enter and exit the stage, where to stand when they are on view, and what to do while they are in place. Directing the rehearsal is the Celebrant, the event planner, or location coordinator. Importantly, there should be one knowledgeable guide preparing the many performers for the live show. Much like rehearsing a play, a wedding rehearsal is about making sure everything we have planned on paper will work practically in the way we want and in the space that has been chosen. It is common for the shape and size of the venue to require subtle adjustments to what has been previously anticipated.

What then are the factors to consider when deciding whether or not to hold a wedding rehearsal?

Number in the wedding party

The more people in the wedding party the more likely is the need for a wedding rehearsal. If the ceremony involves only the couple, a best man, and a maid of honor, you almost certainly don't need a formal rehearsal. If you have more than three each of groomsmen or bridesmaids or you are including parents, ring bearers, or flower girls, in your ceremonial group, a wedding rehearsal starts to look more and more like a good idea. As a rule of thumb, if a wedding party, including the bride and groom, bridesmaids, groomsmen, parents, flower girls, and ring bearers, has the following number, this is what is advised:

Under 5 people: A rehearsal should not be needed unless one is specifically requested.

Between 5 and 10: A rehearsal may be advisable dependant on other factors given below.

Between 10 and 15: A rehearsal is highly advisable. By not holding one, you are taking a risk of mistakes or slip-ups on the day.

Between 15 and 25: A rehearsal is absolutely required. Not to hold one will almost certainly create a noticeable degree of chaos or stress before and during the ceremony.

Over 25: A wedding party of this size is almost certainly too large. You would be strongly advised to tactfully instruct the couple to trim this to a more practical and manageable number.

The complexity of the procession

The more complex the choreography of the entrances and exits of the wedding party the more practice and instruction will be required. If a groomsman must escort a parent, and then double back to his position, or if a child ring bearer must hand off the rings before being seated, a run through before the day can be critical in putting these participants at ease.

The complexity of the ceremony

Many ceremonies involve individuals moving to different positions throughout the proceedings perhaps to perform an action such as a unity ritual. Discovering exactly how this will work in practice, given the realities of the venue space, greatly ensures things will go as desired under the stresses of the formal occasion.

The choice of venue

Some venues are designed specifically for the performing of ceremonies. Other locations can have a shape, size, or design that presents unexpected challenges. This is particularly true of weddings held in private homes or in gardens. The best way to ensure your ideas for orchestrating the key players are possible, or practical, is to rehearse within the space itself, and make adjustments that you find are needed.

The experience of the wedding party

Though less important than some other variables, experience can be the deciding factor where parties are not sure if a rehearsal is needed. If the wedding party consists only of adults, many of whom have been involved in previous ceremonies, a rehearsal is slightly less important than if your plans involve children or if the participants lack confidence or prior experience.

The extra cost of the rehearsal

It is undeniable that rehearsals can cause an increase in expense. As a professional Celebrant, you will be almost certainly charge an additional fee for attending the rehearsal. It is a separate event almost always held on a different day to the ceremony. When performing a rehearsal, you are obviously unable to perform any other event at that time. A rehearsal also very clearly involves extra time and work. Such work should be compensated accordingly. It is possible for a couple to hold a rehearsal without the presence of the Celebrant, but this is always less complete and less effective. The couple may have to cover extra costs for transporting and housing the rest of the wedding party. You should work with the couple to decide whether the cost of the rehearsal outweighs the cost of unexpected problems of dangerously unprepared participants on the day.

The final decision on the need for rehearsing should always remain with the bride and groom. However, uncertainty on this choice is usually a sign that a rehearsal is needed. Any couple is, to some extent, taking a gamble by not holding one. A few carefree couples quite enjoy a splash of the unexpected on their day, but if you want to ensure everybody knows the job they are expected to perform, and the role they have to play, the only way to be confident is to hold a rehearsal.

2.21 - Running a Wedding Rehearsal

When beginning a wedding rehearsal, it is important to gather all the parties and introduce them to each other. You should then ensure that each individual fully understands their role.

It is vital to make every participant aware that they must pay strict attention during the rehearsal. Many participants become easily distracted. You may wish to carry a whistle, or a small bell, to recapture the attention of wayward participants. Alternatively, you can remind them that by not paying attention they are usually delaying the much anticipated rehearsal dinner.

You should begin by examining the venue space, and position the participants as they will be during the main events of the ceremony after the processional but before the recessional. You will want to make sure that the arrangement of the participants creates a nicely balanced pattern pleasing to the eye.

Bridesmaids and Groomsmen will ask how they should stand during the ceremony. In most cases the women will have been given flowers to hold. They should hold these in a relaxed fashion, with arms slightly bent, with the base of the flowers at their navel. For the men, you should suggest a strong stance with the right hand placed on the left wrist. Occasionally, you will hear this suggested as left over right. However, a right on left is better for covering watches. You do not want guests to spend the ceremony reviewing the timepieces of the groomsmen or being blinded by an unfortunate light reflection caused by a watch lens. It is most important that everyone stands in harmony with the others.

Younger ring bearers and flower girls should be assigned seats in the front rows to walk to once they have completed their duties.

The bride and groom should be instructed to create a "triangle" of attention with the Celebrant at the start of the ceremony. They should be partially facing the Celebrant and partially facing each other. They will turn to face each other for the vows, also and the exchange of rings, later in the proceedings.

Once you have everyone placed as they will be during the main parts of the wedding ceremony, it is easier to first practice the recessional. Ensure each participant knows where there are required to be positioned and beside whom they are supposed to stand. Starting with the recessional of the bride and groom, choreograph the exit of the other individuals. Instruct them in the cues they will be looking for, either musical or visual, to begin their exit. Encourage them to move slowly, and with grace, dignity, and rhythm.

Occasionally you will be asked to include the parents in the recessional. If so, you should give a gentle nod for them to rise and leave at the appropriate time. In most cases you will ask the bride's parents to recess before the parents of the groom.

Once you have practiced the recessional, call everyone to order and ask if they have any questions. If they feel confident, you can begin to rehearse the most difficult part; the processional.

Line everyone up in the order they plan to enter. This is then the time to give them "the talk". They should be instructed that they must remain silent before they enter. They should have removed any "bulging items" such as wallets, phones, or keys from their pockets. They should be reminded that the paying of attention is critical on the day.

When you are certain that you have everyone's attention, you should create a line-up of those who will enter starting with the first. At this point, you should ask each to take a moment to memorize who they are stood with, beside, in front of, and behind. You should repeat these instructions during every run through.

You should then begin your first run through of the procession. Ask everyone to begin their entrance only when they are signaled. Instruct everyone to walk slowly.

During the processional there may be places where individuals or groups need to pause in order to allow for pictures to be taken. Watch for these needs and allow for them. Photographers are almost never present for a rehearsal and, if you have prepared for this, be sure to let the photographer know when you meet with them on the day.

As you begin each processional run, remind the participants to smile. Their smile should be a gentle and relaxed one that is not a grimace.

Walk the party through the processional and ensure they retake the positions you set for them at the start of the rehearsal.

Once you have everyone in their starting positions, run through the events of the ceremony itself and then do a second run through of the recessional.

At this point in the rehearsal you will often find you need to call the group to order. Have them take their pre-processional places once again, and take them through another full run through of the proceedings. During this time you will iron out any questions and problems which may have been created by the space or the group.

Finally, you should ask the group to collect for a final line-up and I would recommend a "speed run through". This is an old theatrical technique, whereby getting performers to do things very quickly they more easily memorize their moves and positions. This can also be a fun way to end the rehearsal before you leave for the day.

Do not forget that the performance of a rehearsal is a separate booking to the officiating of the ceremony, and you should be compensated accordingly. Most Celebrants ask a third to a half of their main ceremony fee for attending and coordinating a rehearsal.

2.22 - On the Day

When you arrive to perform a ceremony, it is important to remember that you are part of a *team*. A wedding day is almost always created by a group of professionals working together to build the event and focused on the needs of the bride and the groom.

I strongly recommend arriving at a venue in very good time, perhaps as much as an hour before the ceremony is scheduled to begin. This will enable you to coordinate with the other professionals and the wedding party. It will also allow you to adapt to any adjustments in the wedding plan. Perhaps most importantly, on many occasions an early arrival will give you sufficient time to ensure the needs of the paperwork, and other required formalities, are addressed.

Tip: In the course of you interview with the bride and groom, you should establish the color scheme of the occasion. There will be times when this is an unknown factor before your arrival. This is the very best reason for wearing neutral colors. For male Celebrants who choose to wear ties, a trick to overcome this problem is to travel with a selection in different patterns and colors. On arriving at the ceremony, find out the color which is being worn by the bridesmaids. Their clothing will tell you everything you need to know about the tie you should then choose.

2.23 - Understanding your Legal Obligations

Aside from performing the ceremony, it is important to understand your legal obligations as a Celebrant. An important part of your role is to guide a couple through the process of obtaining a license for their marriage.

In the United States the applications and registrations of marriages are administered by civic functionaries. You should make yourself completely familiar with these processes for every region in which you intend to practice. You should be aware of which documents must be obtained and how these should be returned following the ceremony. Failure to do so could find you facing a fine or a criminal prosecution.

As much as with the ceremony, the couple will be looking to you for guidance in matters of the law pertaining to their marriage. Later in this book you will find outlines of the current legal rules, and processes, applicable to marriage in every part of the United States. However, it is important that you continue to monitor local marriage laws, as these often change from year to year.

Tip: It is often more efficient to obtain any signatures you require before the ceremony. At that time, there are often a few minutes of waiting which can be utilized. Following the ceremony, there can be a need for photography and a desire to celebrate. That can make it hard to steal a moment with the right individuals. From a legal point of view, it makes no difference whether you get the pen on the paper before or after the ceremony, but getting it early can make your life easier on the day.

2.24 - Wedding Cancellations

There will be occasions when you take a booking to perform a ceremony but where the relationship breaks down before it takes place. From a business viewpoint, this is the best reason for taking a deposit for securing your time. All other wedding professionals do so, and it is an excellent practice. A deposit is not just an advance on your fee, but it is a security against your having to turn away other bookings. It does not, however, give you any responsibility to ensure a couple's relationship makes it to the aisle.

The breakdown of an engagement, and the subsequent cancelation of a wedding, is a tragic and emotional event. However, your contract should clearly state that your deposit is not refundable in such circumstances.

When informed of any cancellation, you may be faced with a bride or groom in an extreme emotional state. Your job at this time is not to act as a therapist. As a Humanist, and as a decent human being, your obligation is to act out of kindness and sympathy and with great empathy. As a professional, your job is to act in a correct and appropriate manner.

Unless you are a qualified relationship counselor, you absolutely must not attempt to mediate between or reconcile a couple. The correct response is to express regret and to offer your consultation on any relevant matters limited to your role in the ceremony only if this may be of use. I have found it useful to keep a cancelled booking as "provisional" on my books for several weeks following a cancellation, as it is not unknown for a couple to change their minds once again and decide to continue with their marriage. To charge a second booking fee at such times can be especially harsh when dealing with people in such an emotional situation. However fond of a couple you may become, you must remain a professional, and guard your reputation as such. Never put yourself in a professionally compromising situation when dealing with a client.

2.25 – Pre-marital Education

As one of your services you may decide to offer a "Marriage Educator" role. This is different from a counseling service, as you are only offering to educate on skills rather than resolving relationship issues through reparative, or psychological, means. You must never misrepresent your professional qualifications.

You can discover more about training as a marriage educator by visiting
http://www.marriagecenters.com.

2.26 - Dealing with a Crisis

A wedding is a highly charged emotional situation. As an experienced professional, it is inevitable that members of any wedding party, and many other wedding vendors, will look to you in a time of crisis.

Sometimes, a wedding crisis can occur because of a logistical breakdown. Wine may not have been delivered. Tablecloths may not fit. Flowers may not be as promised. In those situations, the very best option is to stay out of the way, and let other professionals resolve those issues.

It is important to understand that, as a professional, you have been hired to perform a specific task, and that, as long as you are fulfilling your own remit, you have no professional concern with other matters.

It is natural to want to step in and be of aid in times of adversity. However, it is important to take time to understand when this is helpful and when it is not. A wedding is much like a machine in that many parts work together to create a successful outcome. If you step outside your own area to attempt to correct a problem you may make that problem worse.

It is characteristic of weddings that any problem will seem like a major crisis. In actual fact, almost all problems encountered on any wedding day will have a simple solution. Your skill should be to know when you should step in to offer aid, but more importantly you should know when you should step out of the way and let others work. Like you they have probably seen a great deal of challenges, and they will have a few professional tricks up their sleeves.

You may encounter scenes of familial breakdown. Emotions between family members are often at their highest during a wedding. It is important always to remain impartial and remember two important points:

1. The day is about the couple, their wishes, and their bond.

2. Your job is to ensure the ceremony goes ahead as planned, not to heal family feuds.

In becoming ordained as a Humanist Celebrant, you should have shown you have a good level of judgment and a strong understanding of Humanist principles. If you stick to these in the most chaotic hours you will not go far wrong, and you will be acting in the professional manner expected by those who issued your ordination certificate.

2.27 - Understanding and Responding to Spiritual Differences

It is extremely rare for a Humanist Celebrant to preside at a wedding ceremony where *all* those present are Humanists or Atheists. More commonly, there will be an array of spiritual viewpoints present, and some in attendance that are devout in their supernatural beliefs.

It is important to understand, and be confident in, your own spirituality, and respect the opinions of others. However, if you act according to the Humanist ideals of empathy, positivity, love, and a true respect for life many believers will also find a positive spiritual fulfillment in the words you offer.

Most importantly, the words and sentiments expressed in every ceremony you oversee should be positive. If you help build every occasion to resonate with the love of the couple, the hardest heart should find they warm to the day rather than anger because their own faith positions are not fully referenced.

2.28 - Your Celebrant Kit

As you start to work professionally, you should begin to create a Celebrant "kit". This is a collection of items and tools you carry with you to events. Some useful acquisitions you might consider include:

- Notebook
- Receipt book
- Tissues
- Pens (Black x 3)
- E-card reader for payments
- Business cards (x 20)
- A copy of your ordination certificate
- Blank questionnaires
- Blank contracts
- Breath mints

2.29 - Your Wedding Day Book

You will need a copy of your ceremony from which to read your words. Some Celebrants choose to read their text from a printed source, and I believe that is the most reliable. Others choose to read from an electronic device such as a tablet.

If choosing to read your ceremony from an electronic device, ensure it is suitably charged and that the screen will not seem dull under the light of the venue.

If using a printed source, you will need a tasteful, and professional, cover for your pages. Some Celebrants choose a high quality binder. Another excellent option is a smaller "portfolio", where the words of your ceremony are used in place of pictures. Your binder should ideally be black or in a muted color. It is a good idea for any binder or portfolio to have internal plastic covers. These will give protection for your pages and provide extra weight and control in a windy outdoor setting.

Create the text for your book in a large font. Space the words as for speech rather than in written paragraphs. You may wish to underline words to which you intend to give special emphasis.

Tip: Many individuals have complicated names. Write each name in your book as it should be spoken.

2.30 - Getting Paid

Perhaps the least romantic part of life as a professional Celebrant is the act of being paid. Asking a couple for a check immediately before or after a ceremony can be a hugely uncomfortable experience. This can be better handled by making a polite agreement with a couple, before the day, to pass any payment through a third party such as the wedding planner or coordinator. A better policy still is to settle any outstanding amount long before the day. Many couples may prefer this for budgetary reasons.

Try to offer as many payment options as possible. You can offer payment online or through a card reader attached to your cell phone. Both PayPal and Square offer a free reader and a reasonable rate for handling electronic payments. Be sure to carry a receipt book in your kit in case a paper receipt is requested.

2.31 - Networking

The cornerstone of building your Celebrant business is *networking*. You should look at connecting your business, online and directly, with other wedding professionals. Create business cards and carry them with you at all times, and try to swap them with those of every other professional when you are working at an event. If you recommend the professionals you are impressed by, they will very likely recommend you. Never underestimate the importance of building connections and friendships in the wedding business.

Tip: It is a good practice to keep a "Vendor Book". It is common for a Celebrant to be asked to recommend other vendors such as musicians and photographers. In the course of performing ceremonies, you will have a chance to assess the abilities, and professionalism, of others you meet. It can be useful to keep a record, perhaps in a book or file, of those you would be happy to recommend. Just as importantly, it can be useful to keep a second list of those you would rather avoid working with again. Although almost all wedding professionals you meet will be a pleasure to work with, there are unfortunately a few rotten apples in the barrel who you may wish to avoid a second time around.

2.32 - Knowing When to Exit

The ceremony and the paperwork are completed. What then becomes the role of the Celebrant? It is time to say goodbye and tactfully depart. You may find you are asked to stay after the ceremony, but despite the temptation to celebrate there are a number of reasons to decline such gracious offers.

Though your official duties may be complete, you are still "on duty". You are still representing both yourself and Humanist Celebrants everywhere. Your behavior will be scrutinized, and one slip could ruin your reputation and also your chances for an excellent testimonial.

In most cases you will be among strangers you will never see again. If you choose to stay, this can make conversation hard in an environment based on community bonds.

Your best option may be to shake the grooms hand, hug the bride, and bid all a very fond farewell. This is with the understanding that they know where to find you should they have any follow up questions after the day.

2.33 - Post Ceremony Follow Up

You may be asked by the couple, or family members, to send a presentation copy of your ceremony to a home address following the events of the wedding day. You may decide to charge extra for this or factor this expense into your fee.

Some couples will not understand the difference between a marriage license and a marriage certificate. They may contact you some months after the event anticipating that you act in a government capacity. You should be kind and instruct any individual on where to go to find the correct government agency for their needs.

Part Three: Funerals and Memorials

3.1 - Humanist and Non-Religious Funerals and Memorials

Many of the skills you develop, in your function as a Humanist or Non-Religious Wedding Celebrant, will be equally useful in the performance of other types of ceremonies. The talents of public speaking, working with clients and other vendors, working in highly emotional situations, and creating and structuring a ceremony can be adapted to the celebration of many of life's milestones.

There is a growing demand in the United States for end-of-life services which primarily reflect the past, and personality, of the individual whose life has ended rather than conforming to the traditional prayers and formulas required in religious funerals or memorials. Faith-based end-of-life ceremonies can be hugely impersonal or worse at painful odds with the true personality, and spiritual opinions, of the deceased.

A *funeral*, by definition, implies the presence of the deceased, either as a corpse or in the form of an urn containing ashes. A *memorial* takes place without a physical presence and often after the friend or family member has been interred. As a Humanist Celebrant, you will almost certainly be asked to officiate many more memorials than funerals or interments. For Humanists, the human body is often considered merely a natural form of no spiritual or sacred value after life has been extinguished.

The object of all these services is to provide a cathartic experience for loved ones. This should be their opportunity to express their emotions, and revisit their fondest memories of the deceased. In doing so, they are celebrating the life, achievements, and the legacy of someone significant to those around them. In this regard, a Humanist "end of life" celebration can be perhaps the most genuine healing ceremony for those in grief.

3.2 - What is a Humanist Memorial?

A Humanist memorial is a celebration of the life and legacy of an individual. For Humanists, there is no reference to a "passing on", or "moving on", to some concept of afterlife. In fact, such concepts are often seen as offensive to Humanists because they seem to diminish or dilute the value of the life that has been led. Terms such as "going to a better place", "reward", or perhaps worst of all, "home going", imply that the life we have assembled to mourn and celebrate was in some way inferior to some other vague notion of existence for which there is no basis in evidence. In preparing a Humanist memorial service it is vital that you avoid those concepts or allusions. Death should be seen as a part of life, a natural process, and only discussed in those terms.

A Humanist memorial should be a positive event. We should focus on the very best in the life of the deceased and on the moments of greatest success, love, and laughter. Too often a religious ceremony emphasizes a life of pain, tears, and sorrow. This is done to promote the concept of an afterlife as something superior and therefore desirable. It can be clearly observed that treating death as a chance to celebrate life is far healthier during the grieving process and allows family and friends to return to normal life more quickly and with less psychological trauma. All these factors should be foremost in the mind of any Humanist Celebrant preparing and performing a memorial.

3.3 - The Difference between "In Need" and "Pre-planning"

There are two types of "end of life" planning process in which you may be asked to participate. Although they are both concerned with the creation of a funeral or memorial service, these can involve different skills and approaches.

3.4 - In Need Preparation

An "in need" situation occurs after someone has died. In this case, you will be working with a family, or their representative, to create the ceremony. The service venue may already be booked, perhaps through a Funeral Home or other appropriate location, and you may find yourself working with Funeral Directors on the coordination of the day. In order to serve these needs you should be available at short notice and have flexible hours.

Although you will be dealing with clients experiencing some very painful emotions, if a family has decided on a Humanist or Secular ceremony it is because they are looking to accentuate the positive aspects of the deceased's life and celebrate both their memories and legacy. You should be prepared, when asking questions to gather information, always to enquire about and accentuate the positive. You will want to learn about family bonds, personal success, living passions, stories, and triumphs. A Humanist outlook does not, however, seek to distort the experience of life or promote unrealistic ideals. We accept that no one leads a life without trials and setbacks. It is possible and desirable to use such trials to color and emphasize the triumphs of life, and those can provide anecdotes and references which can make for some of the most cathartic and heartwarming parts of the ceremony.

In preparing for this type of event you are not trying to condense a life into a service only you will perform, but rather to seek ways to facilitate a group to best contribute to, and take part in, the ceremony. Remember that with a memorial your role will be more to preside over the ceremony rather than to perform it. You are looking for the best individuals to participate actively throughout the different sections of the event.

You should also give regular thought to controlling the flow and length of the proceedings. When considering the flow, give thought to a rough timeline of the life of the deceased. Ideally, recollections from earlier times, perhaps from school friends, should come before stories of later life. Those closest to the deceased should be given the opportunity to close the period of recollections. An ideal length for a memorial service is around an hour.

The Initial Contact

When first contacted by family, friends, or a representative of the deceased it is important to first discover the time and place of the ceremony. You should immediately check your calendar to ensure you are available. You should then arrange a time for the consulting interview as soon as is convenient and in a suitable location. Unlike the discussion of wedding plans, a public location is almost never appropriate for the planning of a funeral or memorial. It is important during this first enquiry to gather the basic facts about the deceased: name, age, gender, and date of death. More personal details are best gained face to face, but where these are offered at the first contact you should take careful notes to use later.

Pricing

Discussions of pricing and payments are never comfortable, and this is especially so in matters of death and memorial arrangements. However, as a professional, it is important to ensure that your costs are covered. If the subject is treated with tact and respect, the clients will understand you are acting in a dignified and professional manner. As with other kinds of ceremony, the price you ask may vary based on location. You should certainly factor in your travel expenses. In 2015 the I.R.S. stipulated business rate for travel is $0.575 a mile. Do not forget to calculate the cost as a round trip. You may wish to reduce your price if you have a personal familiarity with the deceased or their family. The base amount that you charge for planning and performing a memorial may vary by region, but this will usually fall somewhere between $200 and $500. As with weddings, it is wise to examine the market to ensure you have some parity with other Celebrants.

Contract

When providing "in need" services there can be a very short time between the booking and the ceremony. For this reason, you may decide not to ask for a deposit. However, a contract is always important when conducting business as a professional. A general contract for the performing of a ceremony should be sufficient. I have included a basic example of a contract later in this book. It is most important to clarify exactly who will be responsible for paying your balance and ensuring both parties are fully aware of when and how that balance will be paid. As with all ceremonies, I recommend collecting all outstanding payments prior to the event, as this can make for the cleanest conclusion to your engagement.

The Consulting Interview

At the consulting interview your job is to listen and then to advise. Where a family has chosen a Humanist or Non-religious memorial to honor the wishes of the deceased, they may still have questions about Humanism in a broader context or about your own personal religious outlook. You should be fully prepared to answer these questions.

Much of the consulting interview may be more freeform than you are used to with other types of ceremony planning. The family will likely be keen for you to know as much as possible about the life and achievements of the departed as well as the "great tales" of their living years. You should take as many notes as possible, and look for themes and highlights which you might allude to in your opening words. It is critical, however, that your opening words do not give any "spoilers" regarding the stories or references other speakers are likely to share during the ceremony. Always remember that your primary role will be as a facilitator for the commemoration and grieving of others.

Be sure to establish the correct pronunciation of the name of the deceased and most importantly how they were known to those closest to them. Discover if they had a "pet name" or nickname. Establish the age at which they passed the important landmarks in their life. Make a careful note of the roles they were best known for, both professionally and personally, as a husband, wife, parent, grandparent, son, daughter, co-worker, or other notable place in the community.

By the end of the interview you should have enough information that you will be able to put together a draft order of ceremony, and to know the names, roles, and contact information for the proposed speakers. Be ready to connect with the venue to coordinate on any technical or logistical requirements.

Do not hesitate to stay in touch with your primary contact, and the venue personnel, to ensure arrangements are coming together as planned. As with the run up to all your professional engagements, you should remain available for contact by the parties involved.

3.5 - Pre-planning with the Living

For those with Humanist or Non-religious outlooks on life, it can be important to plan for a final celebration which will reflect this rather than having the memorial distorted by a default religious ceremony. When many United States citizens die, the short planning period, combined with community assumptions, can often lead to a default Christian service. For those who then attend, intensely aware that such an occasion far from represents the deceased, the prayers and platitudes of faith and an afterlife can be uncomfortable, insulting, or disturbing, and these are frequently damaging to the grieving process.

With pre-planning you are helping an individual to consider, and then specify clearly, their own wishes for their memorial. The elements of the ceremony you will discuss with them will be mostly the same, though the interview experience is often a much lighter one. The pre-planning experience for the client is often a surprisingly pleasant opportunity to remember and revisit their life and loves. They can then take time to consider how these aspects could best be commemorated. A pre-planned funeral or memorial service can also greatly assist loved ones with the many difficult decisions which must be made at the end of life.

There is often a discomfort, especially in Western countries, with preparing a memorial for oneself, as we still have a great many taboos surrounding death. There is also the often stated truism that "memorials are for the living, rather than the dead". Though such a statement may have some validity, a ceremony that truly reflects the deceased, and which carries some of their own voice, can be far more beneficial to the grieving process of those attending as compared to one which only reflects the views and outlooks of the mourners.

It is important, within local Humanist communities, to promote the idea of pre-planning for a Humanist death as close in importance to living a Humanistic life. If you are willing to offer the service, you can help to produce and maintain records of their wishes, and be prepared to officiate when the day arrives. This is not, however, a role every Celebrant will feel comfortable with. Just because you are a Celebrant, this does not demand that you must offer every service, or type of ceremony, that can be performed or which may be requested. It is absolutely acceptable to politely and respectfully refuse to perform any ceremony where a request is outside your personal boundaries or comfort zone.

Funeral Homes usually offer pre-planning services which encompass all logistical aspects of the process. In preparing your plan you need often only concern yourself with the organization of the ceremony. Where and when a Funeral Home has been chosen you should be ready to contact them, and introduce yourself as the chosen officiant for that particular individual. You will find most Funeral Directors are very friendly and highly accommodating.

The Initial Contact

Although there are individuals who like to plan far in advance for every eventuality, most pre-planning will take place close to the end of life. Many requests for your services may come through the local Humanist or "Freethought" groups. They may also come from the recommendations of friends or from previous clients. When contacted, your primary goals are to make the prospective client fully aware of your terms of service and then to set up a time for the consulting interview.

Pricing

The amount you charge for preparing a memorial service is very much a matter for your personal discretion. In some cases you may wish to waive a planning fee until such time as the ceremony is fully contracted or has been performed. This is one of the Humanist Celebrant duties which you may feel goes beyond immediate financial reward. If you choose to charge a fee for your time, and for producing the paperwork, you should decide if this will be deducted from your price when the ceremony takes place or if it will be charged as a separate service. A reasonable price for pre-planning as a stand-alone service might be an amount between $70 and $100.

Contract

For pre-planning as a stand-alone service you may wish to quote a price and then accept payment at the consulting interview. Alternatively, you may choose to invoice the client when you deliver the final draft. If the pre-planning is sufficiently close to the time of death as to form part of an ongoing arrangement process you may wish to provide a contract to the client or their representatives that covers both the planning and the performance of the ceremony. You should then decide if you will charge separately for the planning and the ceremony or if you will take a deposit, and then provide an invoice for the balance, just before the ceremony is to be performed. It is wise to complete any financial transactions relating to any ceremony before the event takes place. This makes for the cleanest conclusion to your dealings with the client.

The Consulting Interview

The consulting interview may be held at the client's home, a retirement home, or in a hospice or hospital. The ideal location for discussing memorial pre-planning is in a place with guaranteed privacy, and either alone with the client or with the presence of one close family member or friend. You should allocate at least an hour for discussion, but be prepared to spend more time if needed. The planning process is a delicate one and can involve some time reminiscing and viewing family albums. You should not rush the interview.

Your goal, during the interview, is to arrive at a set of wishes which can be clearly communicated to those with the difficult task of executing them. This will include family and friends as well as other end-of-life professionals. You should talk over the structure and options for the memorial ceremony, and take as many notes as possible. You should aim to leave with enough information to allow you to write a complete ceremony plan on a single page with accompanying pages providing details and notes.

Completing the Process

Once you have gathered all the required information, you should write up your notes into a "memorial plan". This should include full details the client's wishes with regard to readings, music, ceremonial additions, and all other aspects of the occasion. The client should receive and approve this document. You should be prepared to produce a second draft with revisions if requested.

Once the ceremony plan is approved, you must be certain that all the right people know that the information exists and where it is stored. Discuss this issue with the client. Alongside a will is not the best place to store you pre-planning information, as this may not be accessed and read soon enough following the death. Storing the information in a safe deposit box is also not recommended, as these are often sealed upon death, and the contents are not then accessible for a considerable period of time. A good place for the client to store their wishes is with other immediately important papers such as their birth certificate or passport. You should keep a copy of the plan to be used when the time comes. Be sure all the paperwork contains your full contact details, and that important contacts have easy access to that information.

3.6 - Core Elements of a Memorial

Although one of the great advantages of a Humanistic memorial is the power of flexibility, in both form and style, there are certain elements which are hugely useful, and popular, as well as expected in a modern memorial ceremony.

3.6a - Opening Words

As with a wedding, the two key roles of the Celebrant, in their opening words, are to welcome those attending, and explain the nature of what is about to take place. Although you may wish to say a few words of your own about the deceased, it is vital that you do not give away any "spoilers" regarding the anecdotes and references others are likely to offer during the rest of the ceremony. Always remember that, when officiating a memorial, your primary role is as the *facilitator* for the commemorations and grieving of others.

3.6b - Personal Statements and Recollections

At the core of a Humanist memorial service are the statements, recollections, comments, and stories given by family and friends. These come in two forms: the pre-arranged eulogy or address, and the spontaneous comments or recollections offered on the day.

You will need to be careful, when planning your line up of speakers, to allocate time in a manner which suits your arrangements as well as the limits set by the venue. A good time limit for any funeral or memorial service is around one hour from the opening statement to the final words.

A balance should be made between allowing each speaker the opportunity to say all they need and avoiding overrun. Some speakers will inevitably take longer than expected to deliver their thoughts and recollections, while others may be surprisingly brief and concise.

3.6c - Pre-planned Recollections

In the case of pre-planned ceremonies, the client may have strong wishes as to those they would like to give an address on the day. For "In Need" situations, the family and friends will be able to suggest those best able to speak. Do not be surprised if immediate family members decide they are unable to speak at a funeral or memorial. It is incredibly difficult for a spouse to give a eulogy for someone so close.

Those who decide they are able to speak should be guided as to the length of the address they are being asked to give. Six to Seven minutes is the ideal length for an address or eulogy.

3.6d - Spontaneous Statements

There may be friends or family members who decide at the last moment that they wish to say a few words about the deceased. It is useful to allocate a short segment of time to allow for this if the other plans allow. You should not, ideally, stop any who plan to speak from doing so, and you should always ensure that the most important, and closest, speakers have the opportunity to close the reminiscences.

3.6e - Music

Music can be incredibly important to the tone and feel of a ceremony. As Humanists, we would hope for secular contributions which have a special resonance with the life and personality of the deceased whether it was a favorite tune or because the lyrics and style reflect certain aspects of their life. When pre-planning, you will find this is one element many individuals have already considered at some point in their lives.

Music at a funeral or memorial can be purely instrumental or with accompanying lyrics. It can be a live performance or pre-recorded. Almost all Funeral Homes, and many rented venues, have the ability to play pre-recorded music. At a minimum, you should consider a short selection music which can be played as guests are entering and then another as they depart the main ceremony location.

Where there is a member of the family, or a close friend, with musical abilities, whether through instrument or song, it can be a very personal touch to offer them the chance to play at the ceremony.

Tip: As politely as possible, it is worth assessing the level of skill of any amateur musician considered for the ceremony. It is not unknown for an "unaccomplished" musician to provide uncomfortable moments, or unwanted amusement, for which a ceremony may be solely remembered later by those in attendance.

If it is felt appropriate, it can be a nice addition to include a song to be sung by all those in attendance. For a Humanist ceremony, hymns, or any other songs concerned with an afterlife, are highly inappropriate. A group song should strongly resonate with the life of the deceased and ideally be familiar to most of those present.

3.6f - Readings

Many choose to incorporate readings into a memorial service. These can be read by the Celebrant, but it is by far preferable if they are given by a friend or family member. Where a memorial is pre-planned, it may be that the deceased will write a few words to be read to the guests. In our technological age, there is also the option for the deceased to record an audio or video message. Where such a recording is due to be played, those attending should be given some warning as this can be an overwhelming experience for some.

A reading may be a favorite piece of prose or poetry enjoyed by the deceased or something that captures their life and legacy. It is preferable, in a Humanist memorial, that readings be positive in nature and not make mention of a transition to any form of afterlife.

3.6g - A Moment of Silence

Many choose to add a moment of silence during a memorial. In faith based ceremonies this would be a time for prayer. Although making a request for prayer is inappropriate during a Humanist or Non-religious ceremony, a moment of silence can have a useful and appropriate place in the proceedings. These times can be used as moments of contemplation and as a mark of respect for the deceased.

As with other types of ceremony, it will be rare for all those attending to hold Humanist or Non-religious beliefs. Because of this, some guests may choose to use such a moment for silent prayer. This is entirely at their discretion and should not be openly admonished or ridiculed.

3.7 - Ceremonial Additions

One of the great beauties and advantages of Humanist ceremonies is that they are not restrained by strict rules and traditions. The ways in which we can celebrate a life and legacy are limited only by our imagination. Here are a few possible additions you might make to a ceremony:

- A photo collage.
- A tasteful figure, perhaps of whicker or bamboo, clothed or decorated with objects owned by, or highly significant to, the deceased.
- A slideshow.
- Memorial stones. Each guest takes a stone as they enter and writes a brief memory or message upon it and then places it in a basket to be kept by the next of kin.
- Memory notes. Instead of notes placed in a box, you may choose to have symbolic tree which the notes are placed on or beneath.
- Candy bars. If the deceased had a sweet tooth you may wish to offer candy bars for guests to enjoy as they share their memories.
- Seeds, or cuttings, for attendees to take and plant in memory of the deceased.
- Make a recording of the ceremony to share online with those unable to attend.
- If part of a memorial takes place outside you may consider a lantern release.

3.8 - On The Day

On the day of the ceremony you should arrive in good time. Most Funeral Homes have a private room for "clergy" to prepare. Check with the coordinator on the latest time plan for events leading up to, and following, the service. Check that any special requirements have been provided for and that any audio-visual provisions have been met.

It is normal for those closest to the deceased to gather in the "Family Room" or "Family Area" just prior to their entry to the ceremony. At this time you will meet with them and, along with the location organizer if needed, formally introduce yourself and express your personal condolences. You should explain the order of events to those who were not involved in the planning. You should be prepared to answer any questions they may have about the ceremony. You will then lead the entry of the family and, when they are seated and the music has ended, begin your introduction.

At the end of the ceremony, it is appropriate to give instructions to those gathered on where to go for any planned follow-up event or any other helpful information pertinent to the continuation of day. It is useful to ask the venue coordinator or the Funeral Director if they have any special instructions they would like you to give on their behalf.

These are the usual and formal set of circumstances. Many Humanist celebrations, formats, and procedures may be varied and are often more relaxed. Creativity with all ceremonies is definitely to be encouraged.

Part Four: Other Celebrations

In addition to weddings and memorials, there are many other ceremonies a Humanist or Non-religious Celebrant may be asked to perform. Any milestone in the life of an individual, couple, family, group, or community can always be a cause for a formal celebration, and you may well be asked to take the lead in organizing, and officiating, many types of events.

4.1 - Baby Naming and New Life Celebrations

As Humanists, indeed as anyone who treasures humanity, it is hugely appropriate that we celebrate the beginning of a new life with all the potential and promise it holds. Although many religions see a new life as born in sin, and thus requiring a symbolic cleansing with a church blessing before life can begin, Humanists believe that each new life starts free of guilt and with a vast and unknown potential for achievement. Once again the ceremony needs no reference to any supernatural entity. There is also no need to label a child with a specific faith tradition. We should hope they always have an open mind and a kindness of heart.

4.1a - Core Elements of a New Life Ceremony

The Welcome

These are words spoken by the Celebrant explaining why everyone has gathered. You will outline the occasion and explain the setting. It will also describe what is going to happen for those new to the idea of this kind of ceremony for a new born child.

Announcing the Name

This is an important part of the ceremony. Although everyone present will almost certainly already know the name, this is an opportunity to explain the choice and its significance. A lot of thought goes into naming. This is true of all names. Middle names can often have an important family or symbolic significance. It can be appropriate for each of the parents to explain their choice in person rather than have that explanation come solely from the Celebrant.

Parents Promises

Parents' promises to their new child can be somewhat like the wedding vows a couple makes to each other. They can be in the form of repeated lines, answers to questions on the obligations they are making, or perhaps in the form of a short piece of writing which they read aloud. The promises can be made separately by each parent in turn, or they can be made with parent each speaking alternate lines.

Guide Parents Promises

Humanist and Non-religious parents do not appoint "Godparents". Individuals other than the parents are chosen to take the role of a caretaker and mentor and are often referred to as "Guide Parents" or Guardians. The promises and vows that are made are done so to the parents and child rather than in the eyes of any supernatural entity. These statements of promise can be made in much the same way as those of the parents.

The Closing

In closing, the Celebrant will take time to express the hopes of all present for the future of the new born. These thoughts are often ended with a toast and celebration.

4.1b - Possible Additions to a New Life Ceremony

There are many wonderful additions you can make to a New Life ceremony. These include:

- Joining together in song
- A best wishes book
- Releasing sky lanterns
- Creating some handprint art
- Planting a tree
- Filling and sealing a time capsule
- Starting a college fund
- Naming a star

4.1c - How Much To Charge for a New Life Ceremony

It is up to you to decide on your standard fee for preparing and performing a New Life ceremony. The national range at this time appears to fall between $150 and $400. Do not forget to add travel expenses where these are incurred.

4.2 - Invocations

An invocation is a ceremonial statement given at the start of an occasion or gathering. It brings to mind the meaning and spirit of that event. A good invocation should capture the themes of the event and give those attending appropriate concepts to consider. An invocation is usually fairly short in length. It is best at around 100 to 150 words long. It can include a quotation, if appropriate, where this may be useful in illuminating the intention of the statement. A Humanist or Non-religious invocation should always be positive and constructive in tone.

Defining a Humanist Invocation

What are we "invoking" when we write and present a Humanist invocation? Obviously, we are not invoking any supernatural or religious spirit. The best Humanist invocations evoke and celebrate the best in man and nature. They evoke the qualities and aspirations of which we can be proud and which are most relevant to the occasion.

Gathering Information for the Invocation

When approached to give an invocation you should try to gather as much information as possible not just about the date, time, and location but also about the intentions and expectations of the organizers. In addition to wanting a Non-religious text, the organizers will undoubtedly have some key points or issues which they will want you to mention. It is vital to understand the themes of the event which you are being asked to open. For some occasions, the organizers will contribute or supply all or part of the text for the invocation. Do not be afraid to offer comments or suggestions if you feel they are needed. You should also feel able to question any content which you find conflicts with the Humanistic nature of the invocation or which you will be uncomfortable speaking at the event.

What an Invocation is NOT

A Humanist invocation is *not*, under any circumstances, to be used to make open criticism of another religious or political position. An invocation is also not meant as an occasion to proselytize. At all times your words must be positive, constructive, encouraging, and respectful. You will often find yourself addressing a gathering containing individuals of many different viewpoints. At this time you are an ambassador for those with a Humanist or Non-religious point of view. When given the honored position of performing an invocation, your job is to invoke human values to which all reasonable people should be able to relate.

Pricing an Invocation

Many Celebrants choose not to charge for giving an invocation, as these are considered a rare honor and often performed for charitable, or public, institutions. They can also be an excellent source of publicity. However, there is certainly no harm in accepting an honorarium or a free dinner if they are offered.

4.3 - Humanist and Non-Religious Blessings

In creating a Humanist or Non-religious blessing we are not asking for the approval of, or giving thanks to, any supernatural entity. Rather we are asking for all present to consider the importance of an event for their lives, their history, and their community. We are also asking others to contemplate and express their gratitude to the other individuals who contribute their time, energy, and resources for the sake of others. In short, we are asking for the appreciation of human efforts and their significance to a particular occasion. A blessing can often be much like an invocation, though it should generally be less formal. Always positive, it should sum up the values of the occasion and very often ends with a toast or a cheer.

Festive Blessings

There are many wonderful festive occasions throughout the year that can be celebrated without any need to believe in, or call upon, notions of the supernatural. In fact, many festivals are celebrated with greater meaning when viewed in the context of the real human values underlying them such as family, friendship, and a gratitude for the cycles of nature.

Dinner Blessings

Once again, these are much like an invocation though usually less formal. A dinner blessing relates specifically to the food placed before us. Unlike a religious meal blessing, which rather unfairly gives the credit for the feast to an absent deity, a Humanist blessing celebrates the human effort behind the growth and preparation of the food, and this acknowledges the wonders of a truly natural world from which the food is gathered and harvested.

4.4 - Dedications

When work on a project is complete or a key stage in its development is reached, such as with the launching of a boat or the setting of the cornerstone of a building, there is a tradition of saying a few words to mark the occasion. As a Humanist Celebrant, the words you give will not be to thank a deity for the progress and achievement, but rather to praise and acknowledge the human individuals responsible for the accomplishments. You may also wish to offer hope that those achievements will continue to inspire others long into the future.

4.5 - Pet Funerals

A funeral for a beloved pet can easily be as emotional an occasion as that for a friend or relation though it will often be held in a far less formal manner. Much as with your normal memorial role, you may be asked to give opening and closing words. It is useful to have gathered some facts and memories from the owners to use in your text. Your job, when not speaking, is often to act as a facilitator for others to express their feelings and perhaps to give an official signal for any interment or scattering that has been planned.

Part Five: Building a Celebrant Business

As with any business venture, it takes work to be a success. Being a professional Humanist or Non-religious Celebrant is also about far more than just a paycheck. In taking this role, you are helping individuals and families to celebrate unique moments and landmarks in their lives. You are helping others to enjoy the true human basis of values and all those can mean when we honestly embrace them. The role of a Humanist Celebrant is more than a job. You will be acting as a guide and a symbol of the great values which can be expressed without the need for proclaiming faith.

5.1 - Introduction to the Celebrant Business

You will find yourself working with individuals and families at the most emotional times of their lives. As much as marriage or birth, the moments where we say goodbye to the one we love are just as important as any other time in our lives. To help guide them through all these times is a privilege. I hope that everyone taking this role finds human warmth and love in all they do. This is not a standard day job. This is a vocation, and we can make important moments wonderful for those we serve. When we do so, we take home a very true sense of human fulfillment.

5.2 - Your State's Celebrant Requirements

In order to legally perform, or solemnize, marriages, you must fulfill the requirements laid down by each location in which you plan to practice. Later in this volume, you will find a list of those requirements sorted by state. You should familiarize yourself with those sections, and stay alert for any changes that take place over time. Never be afraid to contact your organization of ordination if you have any questions. Your local courthouse should also be able to help clarify the meaning of local statutes.

5.3 - Becoming "Ordained"

Ordination is a crucial step toward performing legal wedding ceremonies. There are several organizations willing, and able, to ordain Humanist and Non-religious Celebrants. It is possible to get a quick online ordination through several web sites. However, it is important to realize that some states may have important concerns about such a fast track process. You are much better advised applying for ordination through an organization which has a more thorough evaluation process and offers membership status.

The Society of Celebrations (www.societyofcelebrations.org) is an organization established to train, and to ordain, Professional Humanist and Non-religious Celebrants. Submitting an application is free, but if accepted the annual fee for membership is currently $75 per year.

The Humanist Society is another organization which gives ordination to Humanist Celebrants. (www.humanist-society.org). Currently, they charge a $40 application fee and $100 per year annual membership.

5.4 - State Registration

In addition to ordination, a number of states require that you register with the local clerk before you may legally perform wedding ceremonies. In most cases, a single registration with one county will ensure you are registered indefinitely across an entire state. In some rare cases, you may need to register in each county. In almost all cases, the extra registration process is an inexpensive formality.

5.5 - Know Your Marriage Laws

The next step to solemnizing marriages is to understand the processes that must be completed by the couple, and by you, with regard to the marriage license. The process, and price, of application varies greatly from state to state as do the obligations of the Celebrant in completing and returning the documents. Later in this volume I have detailed the requirements by state. As with ordination, the local clerk will be very happy to answer any questions you have for their county.

It is important to note that marriage laws can change frequently in each state. At this time, this is especially true with regard to same sex marriage. The cost to the couple for a license application may also be adjusted on a regular basis. As a professional, you should arrange to check your information is up to date, and watch for notifications of important changes.

5.6 - Tax and Small Business Law

When starting a new business of any kind, it is important to ensure you are in compliance with local business and tax laws. In almost all cases, it is a good idea to register your business locally. That should not be an expensive process. It is extremely worthwhile to spend an hour with a good local accountant to discuss the tax rules relating to your business. Where your only income comes from practicing Celebrant duties, you may be entitled to some special tax incentives.

5.7 - Recording Sales, Expenses and Earnings

If you are taking money for services, and spending money on expense items such as gas and dry cleaning, you need to keep a record of these for yourself and most especially for your annual taxes. For a simple set of transactions, you may be able to keep track using a spreadsheet program, such as Microsoft Excel, or an equivalent free program such as Apache OpenOffice.

Once your business begins to grow, and you have significantly more records to keep, you should look to move to a dedicated bookkeeping program such as Intuit QuickBooks. It is surprisingly easy to get started using the company setup "wizards" contained in these programs. Most local community colleges also offer inexpensive courses, from beginner to advanced level, to teach you to use these software packages. Additionally, a good bookkeeping program will have the ability to export your data in a way that smoothly interfaces with the software used by almost all accountants and also by many of the personal tax software packages.

5.8 - Services, Pricing and Payments

In preparing your business, you must decide which services you wish to offer, how much you intend to charge, and how you will take payments.

Choosing your Services

At no time are you obliged to perform every type of ceremony which you are asked for. You may decide you only wish to perform wedding ceremonies or only to officiate at memorial services. Additionally, you should decide which areas and locations you wish to serve. While some Celebrants are willing to travel far, and even stay overnight if requested, others do not wish the strain of a long distance commute. You may decide only to work some months of the year or only at weekends. These are important questions to answer before you begin to market your services and prior to accepting bookings and deposits.

Setting Prices

As with any service, prices for performing ceremonies will vary from location to location. For weddings, prices appear to fall between $200 and $500, with a common rate being $350 for preparing the ceremony and performing it on the day. Where a rehearsal is held on a different day, and is thus a separate event, this can incur an extra fee of around $150. The figures for performing memorials are often similar, though some Celebrants may choose to charge a lower rate for that service, perhaps an amount between $150 to $350. These are merely suggested guidelines, and you should research your own region to see what other Celebrants are charging successfully.

You will almost certainly be travelling to perform ceremonies, and you should seek to be compensated for these expenses. The business vehicle rate given by the I.R.S. in 2015 is $0.575 per mile. Don't forget to calculate your costs as a round trip.

Taking Payments

The more ways you are able to take payments the easier you will make the booking process for your clients. In addition to taking cash and checks, it is now easy to take cards on your phone using a service such as PayPal (www.paypal.com) or Square (www.squareup.com). Your clients may also wish to pay through your website. Your bank may offer a system, such as with Authorize.net, which can be integrated directly into a web page and can give you very good rates for taking payments.

When you accept a booking, it is wise to take a down payment perhaps of $150 for a $350 service. This is insurance against turning down other bookings for the date only to have the original booking fall through. Any deposit should be non-refundable, and this should be stated in your contract. You should ensure that the full balance of any payment for services is received before the start of the ceremony.

Your Contract

If you are doing business professionally, it is wise to lay out an agreement for services in the form of a contract. This should stipulate what is expected by both parties. Later in this volume, I have provided a basic sample wedding contract. It is highly advisable to have a local lawyer look over the contract you create for your business to ensure it conforms to the correct statutes and practices for your location.

5.9 - Choosing a Business Name

Choosing the name you will do business under is a big step, but it can also be an important turning point in setting up your Celebrant practice. You may simply want to use your own given name, or you may have a catchy business name in mind. Here are some factors to consider when deciding the title by which your business will be known.

Should you use the name of a town or state in your business name?

Many Celebrants choose to focus on providing services only in a specific location. If this is true in your case, you may wish to include the name of your area in your business name. Not only does this emphasize that you are a local vender, something many find appealing, but it also helps your result position for online searches by prospective clients looking for your services in that location.

Does your name roll off the tongue in an appealing and memorable way?

The best business names are easy to say, easy to remember, and easy to read on a business card. If you have a given name that is long, hard to pronounce, and hard to spell, then it is a good idea to think of an alternative business name to use in its place. Consider how easy it would be to communicate your business name, domain name, or e-mail address over the phone. You should try your ideas out on friends and family to see if they agree that your choice is clear, memorable, and easy to say for everyone.

Should your name be descriptive?

If you are looking to provide a very specific service, you might consider including that as part of your business name. (e.g. John Smith Officiant, YourTown Wedding Celebrant, Ceremonies by John, etc.)

Is the DBA available?

Many states require you to file a Doing Business As, or D.B.A., and pay a small fee for that registration. Check with your county office, or their web site, for the requirements in your location. You can also find more information from the I.R.S. (www.irs.gov), and the Small Business Association (www.sba.gov).

Is a friendly and catchy domain name available?

In the 21st century, a business name goes hand in hand with a domain name. When choosing a domain name it is important to think about how easy it will be to remember, type, and spell. It is a bad idea to use numbers, hyphens, or words with many possible spelling variations or silent letters.

Most important of all, your domain name must be available to register. Domains are never owned forever after one single payment but are rather registered for a number of years at a time. Of course, you can register year after year, but if you do not renew your domain name you will lose it, and somebody else will have the chance to take it for themselves.

In choosing the type of domain name you will almost certainly be looking of the *.com* suffix, as you will be acting as a business by which you profit. *.org* names are usually taken by non-profit organizations.

To check if the domain name you are interested in is available, or to see possible variations of a name which you might use, visit a well known domain registrar such as GoDaddy (www.godaddy.com).

5.10 - Online Marketing

Creating a Website

Almost every modern business needs a website. Fortunately, the process of creating one is a lot less painful than it was a few years ago. There are many reliable companies who will offer you cheap hosting by the year. Using a Content Management System such as Wordpress (www.wordpress.org), most people who are moderately computer literate can create, and maintain, an effective site to showcase their business. If you choose to use a third party web design company, ask around friends and family for recommendations. The skills, and professionalism, of web designers can vary widely, but as a rough guide you should look to pay around $600-$700, and no more than $1000, for a beautiful and professional looking web site.

Social Media

Whatever our personal opinions of them, Facebook, Twitter, and other social media sites have become part of the toolkit for business marketing. On Facebook you will be seeking to create a "page" for your business, while with a site such as LinkedIn you will be looking to create a "profile". I have placed links to many of the major Social Media sites in the resources section later in this book.

Professional Wedding Site Advertising

There are many sites built specifically to showcase Wedding Professionals. After much trial and experimental marketing, my opinion is that my best investment has been with weddingwire.com (part of the eventwire.com group). It has easily the largest share of the online wedding vendor search market, a great suite of user friendly tools, excellent customer service, and most importantly brings in the customer enquiries. I would like to make it clear that I have taken no money for that endorsement!

Blogging

For the uninitiated, blogging is the posting of short articles, snippets, or updates. In most cases, it is a little like an online diary or commentary. If you have the time and inclination, this can be a great way to post stories and photographs online which showcase your talents. You may also want to post great ceremony ideas as a way to increase traffic to your web site. At the very least, this is a good way to practice your writing skills.

5.11 - Offline Marketing

Networking

Although an online presence will be crucial in building your business, networking is at the heart of becoming established as a Celebrant. A primary marketing goal should be to establish relationships and goodwill with other event professionals who work in your location.

The simplest, and most common, way to network is to exchange contact information, and build a personal rapport with other vendors you meet during the course of your work. These would include venue managers, event organizers, photographers, musicians, caterers, flower providers, and in fact anyone with whom a relationship of mutual recommendation would be beneficial. Always carry a pen and a set of business cards. Keep the cards and numbers you receive and file them away. It is common for a Celebrant to be asked to recommend other types of vendor based on their experiences of them. Be honest in your recommendations. Suggesting a poor quality vendor could also reflect badly on your reputation and any subsequent review you might receive.

Printed Materials

Your key printed material will be your business cards. These are the first items you hand out to others you meet at a ceremony and in the course of any conversation you have about your work as a Celebrant. You should always carry your business cards with you. Additionally, many local businesses may allow you to display your cards on their premises. There is no more important tool in your networking arsenal.

You will want to include certain important information on your business cards: Your name, a description of your job or job title, your business name if different, your telephone number, your e-mail address, and your website address.

Business cards do not need to be an expensive purchase. Websites such as Vistaprint (www.vistaprint.com) can offer excellent deals as well as design templates you can use. A standard batch of 250 cards should be enough to get you started.

If you have some design skills, you might like to create a three-fold flyer to describe your talents and services, and perhaps reproduce some photographs and testimonials.

It is vitally important that you include your full contact information on *every single item of printed material you produce*.

Mailings

You may consider sending a mailing to wedding planners and venues in the area you have decided to cover. A search of any professional listing sites will quickly give you a list of these contacts. A physical mailing, though slightly more costly than a simple e-mail, will enable you to send them a nicely structured letter or flyer, along with business cards, which others can keep to hand. Do not be afraid to reuse, or to adapt, previously written text across your marketing material. Writing an introductory letter can also be a great way to create material which can then be used on your website homepage, and the same is true in reverse. In terms of a return on time invested, however, building your website and creating your business cards should always come before any mail marketing.

5.12 - Building your Professional Kit

Clothing

Although there is no official, traditional, or required attire for a Humanist Celebrant, you will need a reasonable supply of smart, clean, formal wear. If there is a possibility that you may perform several ceremonies in a week, you need to ensure you have enough sets of clothing to cover the times when other outfits are being washed or at the dry cleaners. It is also worth owning separate footwear for the different environments in which a ceremony may take place. Appropriate footwear for a beach, or a park, will be quite different to that suitable for a ballroom or a funeral home.

Tools of the Trade

There are many useful items that you might choose to include in your Celebrant toolkit. In addition to a professional quality book or binder, some items you might consider including in your bag are:

- Notebook
- Receipt Book
- Tissues
- Pens (x3)
- Electronic Card Reader for taking payments on your phone
- Business Cards
- A Copy of your Ordination Certificate, in a plastic cover for protection
- Blank Questionnaire Forms
- Blank Contracts
- Breath Mints

5.13 - Working with Clients

Your Service Questionnaires

When taking the first enquiry from a client, and then conducting your main pre-ceremony interview, it is helpful to have a copy of the usual questions laid out for the appropriate topic. Included in the appendices for this book are examples of enquiry and interview forms for both weddings and funerals.

Meeting Locations

Although you may sometimes be asked to meet at the home of a client, couple, or family, a restaurant or café is also a common choice. When choosing a venue, make sure the ambient noise will be low, that you will have plenty of table room to take notes, and that you and your clients will get all the privacy you need.

5.14 - Continuing Growth

Building Your Skills

As a professional, you should always be looking to expand your knowledge and skills. Take time to read, watch videos online, and embrace any opportunities to practice your public speaking, presentation, and writing skills. Check in regularly with useful web sites, and consider subscribing to news and notice board feeds.

Sharing Your Experiences

As much as you can gain from reading the thoughts, and personal experiences, of others, they can gain a great deal from listening to, or reading about, your life as a professional Humanist Celebrant. Unlike many professions, there is little rivalry among Celebrants, and this is especially true of Humanist and Non-religious Celebrants. We are painfully short of competent and experienced professionals, and there are far from enough to fulfill a rapidly growing demand across the country. By connecting with other Celebrants, you will help to strengthen and grow our community, and perhaps participate in the hugely rewarding process of mentoring a new Celebrant for your region and beyond.

515 - New Celebrant Business Checklist

Suggested stages you may want to pass though on the path to building your Celebrant business:

- Verify Your State's Ordination Requirements.
- Become Ordained.
- Register With Your State or Local Jurisdiction If Needed.
- Learn Your State Marriage Laws and License Process.
- Confirm Your Local Tax and Small Business Laws.
- Create a System to Record your Sales, Earnings, and Expenses.
- Decide on the Services You Will Offer.
- Decide on the Prices You Will Charge.
- Decide on Your Payment and Deposit Policies.
- Create A Contract for Services.
- Decide on Your Company or Professional Name.
- Register Your Name if Required Locally.
- Decide on Your Advertising Budget.
- Register Your Professional Internet Domain Name.
- Ensure You Have the Clothing You Will Need.
- Create a Website.
- Create a Facebook Page.
- Create a LinkedIn Profile.
- Create a Profile on Wedding Wire.
- Have Some Business Cards Printed.
- Put Together Your Celebrant Case or Kit.
- Make Up Your Questionnaires and Enquiry Sheets.
- Set Up a Good Client Filing System.
- Create an Introduction Letter For Venues and Vendors.
- Create a Flyer For Clients.
- Continue To Learn More About Humanism and Ceremonies.

Appendix A: Wedding Celebrant Laws by U.S. State

Alabama

Section 30-1-7

Marriages may be solemnized by any licensed minister of the gospel in regular communion with the Christian church or society of which the minister is a member.

Marriage may also be solemnized by the pastor of any religious society according to the rules ordained or custom established by such society.

Online ordination is not acceptable.

Alaska

AS 25.05.261. Who May Solemnize

(a) Marriages may be solemnized

(1) by a minister, priest, or rabbi of any church or congregation in the state, or by a commissioned officer of the Salvation Army, or by the principal officer or elder of recognized churches or congregations that traditionally do not have regular ministers, priests, or rabbis, anywhere within the state;

(2) by a marriage commissioner or judicial officer of the state anywhere within the jurisdiction of the commissioner or officer; or

(3) before or in any religious organization or congregation according to the established ritual or form commonly practiced in the organization or congregation.

Online ordination is not acceptable.

Arizona

25-124. Persons authorized to perform marriage ceremony; definition

A. The following are authorized to solemnize marriages between persons who are authorized to marry:

1. Duly licensed or ordained clergymen...

For the purposes of this section, "licensed or ordained clergymen" includes ministers, elders or other persons who by the customs, rules and regulations of a religious society or sect are authorized or permitted to solemnize marriages or to officiate at marriage ceremonies.

Arkansas

A.C.A. § 9-11-213 Persons who may solemnize marriages.

Any regularly ordained minister or priest of any religious sect or denomination. You must record your credentials recorded in any county clerk's office of any county.

California

Section 400

Marriage may be solemnized by any of the following who is of the age of 18 years or older and is a priest, minister, or rabbi of any religious denomination.

The laws of the State of California make it unnecessary for persons performing marriages to file credentials with the clerk of the court or with anyone else. The county and state are removed from any responsibility for verification of credentials. The State does not maintain a central registry of members of the clergy. Any such concern for verification is totally at the discretion of the parties to the marriage.

Colorado

C.R.S 14-2-109

A marriage may be solemnized by a judge of a court; by a court magistrate; by a retired judge of the court; by a public official whose powers include solemnization of marriages; by Indian tribe officials; by clergy; by the parties to the marriage.

Connecticut

Sec. 46b-22

All ordained or licensed members of the clergy, belonging to this state or any other state, as long as they continue in the work of the ministry. All marriages solemnized according to the forms and usages of any religious denomination in this state…are valid. All marriages attempted to be celebrated by any other person are void.

Online ordination is not acceptable.

Delaware

Title 13:1 § 106

A clergyperson or minister of any recognized religion.

Online ordination (through recognized religion) is acceptable.

District of Columbia

46-406

For the purpose of preserving the evidence of marriages in the District of Columbia, every minister of any religious society approved or ordained according to the ceremonies of his religious society, whether his residence is in the District of Columbia or elsewhere in the United States or the territories, may be authorized by any judge of the Superior Court of the District of Columbia to celebrate marriages in the District of Columbia.

You must have an endorser from the same religious society, who is currently registered with the Marriage Bureau Section, Family Court. If there is no endorser, you must request the written "Procedures for the Registration of Clergy Without Endorser." Authorization is indefinite for District of Columbia marriage ceremonies.

http://www.dccourts.gov/dccourts/docs/family/marriage.pdf

http://www.dccourts.gov/dccourts/docs/family/register_clergy.pdf

Online ordination is not acceptable.

Florida

Title XLIII Chapter 741.07

All regularly ordained ministers of the gospel or elders in communion with some church, or other ordained clergy, and all judicial officers, including retired judicial officers, clerks of the circuit courts, and notaries public of this state may solemnize the rights of matrimonial contract, under the regulations prescribed by law.

Online ordination is not acceptable.

Georgia

The license shall be directed to...minister, or other person of any religious society or sect authorized by the rules of such society to perform the marriage ceremony...

Hawaii

§572-12

A license to solemnize marriages may be issued to, and the marriage rite may be performed and solemnized by any minister, priest, or officer of any religious denomination or society who has been ordained or is authorized to solemnize marriages according to the usages of such denomination or society.

If you are a minister establishing a new denomination in the State of Hawaii which has no religious affiliation elsewhere and you are the head of the church, submit a letter of recommendation from the members of the Board of Directors or Board of Trustees (signed by each member with his name address and telephone number typed under his signature). In addition, submit a letter stating that you are the head of the church in Hawaii and a xerox copy of the church incorporation papers. An I.D. with a photo, such as a driver's license or state I.D. card must be presented.

This means that you must be commissioned by the State of Hawaii, Department of Health to solemnize marriages. You can call the Health Department at (808) 586-4540.

Idaho

Title 32 Chapter 3:32-303

Marriage may be solemnized by either a . . . priest or minister of the gospel of any denomination.

Illinois

750 ILCS 5/209

[Any minister] in accordance with the prescriptions of any religious denomination . . . Provided that . . . the officiant be in good standing with his religious denomination.

Indiana

IC 31-11-6-1

Marriages may be solemnized by any of the following: (1) A member of the clergy of a religious organization (even if the cleric does not perform religious functions for an individual congregation), such as a minister of the gospel, a priest, a bishop, an archbishop, or a rabbi.

Iowa

595.10.2

A person ordained or designated as a leader of the person's religious faith.

Kansas

Chapter 23 Article 1:23-104a.(b):(1),(2)

Any currently ordained clergyman or religious authority of any religious denomination or society; any licentiate of a denominational body or an appointee of any bishop serving as the regular clergyman of any church of the denomination to which the licentiate or appointee belongs, if not restrained from so doing by the discipline of that church or denomination.

Note: Ministers are required to file credentials or ordination with the judge of a probate court before performing marriages.

Kentucky

KRS 402.050(1)(a)

Marriage shall be solemnized only by: (a) Ministers of the gospel or priests of any denomination in regular communion with any religious society.

Louisiana

RS 9:202

A priest, minister, rabbi, clerk of the Religious Society of Friends, or any clergyman of any religious sect, who is authorized by the authorities of his religion to perform marriages, and who is registered to perform marriages.

Note: Ministers must register with the clerk of the district court of the parish or with the registrar of vital records by providing "an affidavit stating his or her lawful name, denomination, and address".

Maine

Title 19-A Part 2 Chapter 23 §655:1B:1,2,3

Whether a resident or nonresident of this State and whether or not a citizen of the United States: An ordained minister of the gospel; A cleric engaged in the service of the religious body to which the cleric belongs; or A person licensed to preach by an association of ministers, religious seminary or ecclesiastical body.

Maryland

§ 2-406 (2)

A marriage ceremony may be performed in this State by any official of a religious order or body authorized by the rules and customs of that order or body to perform a marriage ceremony.

Massachusetts

Title III, Chapter 207, Section 38

A marriage may be solemnized in any place within the commonwealth by the following persons who are residents of the commonwealth: a duly ordained minister of the gospel in good and regular standing with his church or denomination, including an ordained deacon in The United Methodist Church or in the Roman Catholic Church; a commissioned cantor or duly ordained rabbi of the Jewish faith . . . it may be solemnized by a duly ordained nonresident minister of the gospel if he is a pastor of a church or denomination duly established in the commonwealth and who is in good and regular standing as a minister of such church or denomination, including an ordained deacon in The United Methodist Church or in the Roman Catholic Church; and, it may be solemnized according to the usage of any other church or religious organization which shall have complied with the provisions of the second paragraph of this section.

Churches and other religious organizations shall file in the office of the state secretary information relating to persons recognized or licensed as aforesaid, and relating to usages of such organizations, in such form and at such times as the secretary may require.

Section 39: (Out of State Clergy) a minister of the gospel in good and regular standing with his church or denomination; a commissioned cantor or duly ordained rabbi of the Jewish faith. (There is a $25.00 registration fee with the Secretary of State (617) 727-7030).

Note:

Before performing marriages, ministers are required to apply for a certificate from the state. For applications visit the Commonwealth of Massachusetts website. You must file a copy of your ordination certificate and a statement from the church saying that you are in good standing. Ministers must keep records of all marriages they perform. Also, ministers must return a certificate of the marriage to the town clerk or registrar who issued the marriage license and to the town clerk of the town where the marriage was performed.

If an out-of-state member of the clergy is to perform the marriage, the clergy person must obtain a Certificate of Authorization from the Massachusetts Secretary of the Commonwealth prior to the ceremony. This certificate, which is issued by the Public Records Division of the Secretary of the Commonwealth, is to be attached to the original license and returned to the clerk of the city or town where the license was issued. For further information, contact:

Division of Public Records

Secretary of the Commonwealth

One Ashburton Place, Room 1719

Boston, MA 02108

(617) 727-2836

Officiant for a Day: In Massachusetts, a couple can choose to have a family friend or relative perform their wedding ceremony. In order to become a "Justice of the Peace" for a day, you must fill out an application from the Massachusetts Secretary of the Commonwealth. The process takes 4-6 weeks to complete.

After filling out the application and sending it back, you will then receive a letter from the Secretary of Commonwealth granting permission for the person to perform the wedding ceremony. The letter will give you further instructions to complete the process. There is a $25 fee to apply.

Notary Publics cannot perform weddings in Massachusetts.

Michigan

R.S. of 1846 Chapter 83:551.7,(1)(i),(j):

Marriages may be solemnized by any of the following:

(i) A minister of the gospel or cleric or religious practitioner, anywhere in the state, if the minister or cleric or religious practitioner is ordained or authorized to solemnize marriages according to the usages of the denomination.

(j) A minister of the gospel or cleric or religious practitioner, anywhere in the state, if the minister or cleric or religious practitioner is not a resident of this state but is authorized to solemnize marriages under the laws of the state in which the minister or cleric or religious practitioner resides.

Minnesota

517.04:

Marriages may be solemnized throughout the state by . . . a licensed or ordained minister of any religious denomination.

Mississippi

§ 93-1-17:

By whom marriages may be solemnized.

Any minister of the gospel ordained according to the rules of his church or society, in good standing; any Rabbi or other spiritual leader of any other religious body authorized under the rules of such religious body to solemnize rites of matrimony and being in good standing.

Missouri

451.100:

Marriages may be solemnized by any clergyman, either active or retired, who is in good standing with any church or synagogue in this state. . . Marriages may also be solemnized by a religious society, religious institution, or religious organization of this state, according to the regulations and customs of the society, institution or organization, when either party to the marriage to be solemnized is a member of such society, institution or organization.

Montana

40-1-301:

In accordance with any mode of solemnization recognized by any religious denomination. This means that any licensed or ordained minister can solemnize a marriage so long as it is in accordance in the way of the licensing church.

Nebraska

42-108:

Every preacher of the gospel authorized by the usages of the church to which he or she belongs to solemnize marriages, may perform the marriage ceremony in this state.

Nevada

NRS 122.062:1, 4.

Any licensed or ordained minister in good standing within his denomination, whose denomination, governing body and church, or any of them, are incorporated or organized or established in this state, may join together as husband and wife persons who present a marriage license obtained from any county clerk of the State, if the minister first obtains a certificate of permission to perform marriages as provided in this section and NRS 122.064 to 122.073, inclusive. The fact that a minister is retired does not disqualify him from obtaining a certificate of permission to perform marriages if, before his retirement, he had active charge of a congregation within this state for a period of at least 3 years.

4. A county clerk may authorize a licensed or ordained minister whose congregation is in another state to perform marriages in the county if the county clerk satisfies himself that the minister is in good standing with his denomination or church. The authorization must be in writing and need not be filed with any other public officer. A separate authorization is required for each marriage performed. Such a minister may perform not more than five marriages in this state in any calendar year and must acknowledge that he or she is subject to the jurisdiction of the county clerk with respect to the provisions of this chapter governing the conduct of ministers or other persons authorized to solemnize a marriage to the same extent as if he or she were a minister or other person authorized to solemnize a marriage residing in this State..

Like Ohio, Nevada has very strict marriage licensing laws. Please go to http://www.co.clark.nv.us/clerk/pdf/Forms/NRS_122.pdf for additional instructions. Please do not skip over tip.

New Hampshire

457:31

Marriage may be solemnized...by any minister of the gospel in the state who has been ordained according to the usage of his or her denomination, resides in the state, and is in regular standing with the denomination; by any clergyman who is not ordained but is engaged in the service of the religious body to which he or she belongs, resides in the state, after being licensed therefore by the secretary of state; within his or her parish, by any minister residing out of the state, but having a pastoral charge wholly or partly in this state.

New Jersey

37:1-13:

Every minister of every religion, are hereby authorized to solemnize marriage between such persons as may lawfully enter into the matrimonial relation; and every religious society, institution or organization in this State may join together in marriage such persons according to the rules and customs of the society, institution or organization.

New Mexico

40-1-2:

A person may solemnize the contract of matrimony by means of an ordained clergyman.

New York

Chapter 14:3:11

A clergyman or minister of any religion. According to Section 11 of the Domestic Relations Law, an officiant must be an authorized, officially ordained member of the clergy or a public official in the State of New York such as a mayor, city clerk, deputy city clerk, appointed marriage officer, justice, or judge. In New York City, an officiant must be registered with the City of New York. Ship captains can not perform marriage ceremonies in New York State.

North Carolina

Chapter 51-1

Any ordained or licensed clergymen and justices of the peace.

North Dakota

14-03-09:

Ordained ministers of the gospel; priests; clergy licensed by recognized denominations pursuant to chapter 10-33; and by any person authorized by the rituals and practices of any religious persuasion.

Ohio

§ 3101.08:

An ordained or licensed minister of any religious society or congregation within this state who is licensed to solemnize marriages . . . or any religious society in conformity with the rules of its church, may join together as husband and wife any persons who are not prohibited by law from being joined in marriage.

§ 3101.10 A minister upon producing to the secretary of state, credentials of his being a regularly ordained or licensed minister of any religious society or congregation, shall be entitled to receive from the secretary of state a license authorizing him to solemnize marriages in this state so long as he continues as a regular minister in such society or congregation. A minister shall produce for inspection his license to solemnize marriages upon demand of any party to a marriage at which he officiates or proposes to officiate or upon demand of any probate judge.

You must apply to the secretary of state to receive authorization to perform marriages.

Oklahoma

§43-7: A

All marriages must be contracted by a formal ceremony performed or solemnized in the presence of at least two adult, competent persons as witnesses, by . . . an ordained or authorized preacher or minister of the Gospel, priest or other ecclesiastical dignitary of any denomination who has been duly ordained or authorized by the church to which he or she belongs to preach the Gospel, or a rabbi and who is at least eighteen (18) years of age.

2. The preacher, minister, priest, rabbi, or ecclesiastical dignitary who is a resident of this state shall have filed, in the office of the court clerk of the county in which he or she resides, a copy of the credentials or authority from his or her church or synagogue authorizing him or her to solemnize marriages.

3. The preacher, minister, priest, rabbi, or ecclesiastical dignitary who is not a resident of this state, but has complied with the laws of the state of which he or she is a resident, shall have filed once, in the office of the court clerk of the county in which he or she intends to perform or solemnize a marriage, a copy of the credentials or authority from his or her church or synagogue authorizing him or her to solemnize marriages.

4. The filing by resident or nonresident preachers, ministers, priests, rabbis, ecclesiastical dignitaries or judges shall be effective in and for all counties of this state; provided, no fee shall be charged for such recording.

5. No person herein authorized to perform or solemnize a marriage ceremony shall do so unless the license issued therefore be first delivered into his or her possession nor unless he or she has good reason to believe the persons presenting themselves before him or her for marriage are the identical persons named in the license, and for whose marriage the same was issued, and that there is no legal objection or impediment to such marriage.

Oregon

106.120

Marriages may be solemnized by: Religious congregations or organizations as indicated in ORS

106.150 or

(d) A clergyperson of any religious congregation or organization who is authorized by the congregation or organization to solemnize marriages.

(2) A person authorized to solemnize marriages under subsection (1) of this section may solemnize a marriage anywhere in this state.

106.150 Form of solemnization; witnesses; solemnization before congregation. (1) In the solemnization of a marriage no particular form is required except that the parties thereto shall assent or declare in the presence of the clergyperson, county clerk or judicial officer solemnizing the marriage and in the presence of at least two witnesses, that they take each other to be husband and wife.

(2) All marriages, to which there are no legal impediments, solemnized before or in any religious organization or congregation according to the established ritual or form commonly practiced therein, are valid. In such case, the person presiding or officiating in such religious organization or congregation shall make and deliver to the county clerk who issued the marriage license the certificate described in ORS 106.170. [Amended by 1979 c.724 §5; 2001 c.501 §2] Judges, County Clerks or their Deputies, Justices of Peace, and ministers, pastors, priests, rabbis may perform wedding ceremonies in Oregon.

Pennsylvania

§ 1503

A minister, priest or rabbi of any regularly established church or congregation.

b) Religious organizations.—Every religious society, religious institution or religious organization in this Commonwealth may join persons together in marriage when at least one of the persons is a member of the society, institution or organization, according to the rules and customs of the society, institution or organization.

(c) Marriage license needed to officiate.—No person or religious organization qualified to perform marriages shall officiate at a marriage ceremony without the parties having obtained a marriage license issued under this part. Ministers need to file their credentials with the county clerk's office before solemnizing any marriages.

Rhode Island

§ 15-3-5

Every ordained clergy or elder in good standing may join persons in marriage in any city or town in this state. You must obtain a license to marry from the city or town clerk before solemnizing any marriages.

South Carolina

SECTION 20-1-20

Only ministers of the Gospel or accepted Jewish rabbis and officers authorized to administer oaths in this State are authorized to administer a marriage ceremony in this State.

South Dakota

25-1-30

Marriage may be solemnized by . . . any person authorized by a church to solemnize marriages.

Tennessee

36-3-301 (a) (1)

All regular ministers, preachers, pastors, priests, rabbis and other spiritual leaders of every religious belief, more than eighteen (18) years of age, having the care of souls.

(2) In order to solemnize the rite of matrimony, any such minister, preacher, pastor, priest, rabbi or other spiritual leader must be ordained or otherwise designated in conformity with the customs of a church, temple or other religious group or organization; and such customs must provide for such ordination or designation by a considered, deliberate, and responsible act.

Texas

§ 2.202: a)

The following persons are authorized to conduct a marriage ceremony:

(1) a licensed or ordained Christian minister or priest;

(2) a Jewish rabbi;

(3) a person who is an officer of a religious organization and who is authorized by the organization to conduct a marriage ceremony.

Utah

30-1-6

Marriages may be solemnized by the following persons only:

(a) Ministers, rabbis, or priests of any religious denomination who are:

(i) in regular communion with any religious society; and

(ii) 18 years of age or older;

2) A person authorized under Subsection (1) who solemnizes a marriage shall give to the couple married a certificate of marriage that shows the:

(a) Name of the county from which the license is issued; and

(b) Date of the license's issuance..

Vermont

§ 5144

Marriages may be solemnized by . . . a member of the clergy residing in this state and ordained or licensed, or otherwise regularly authorized thereunto by the published laws or discipline of the general conference, convention or other authority of his or her faith or denomination or by such a clergy person residing in an adjoining state or country, whose parish, church, temple, mosque or other religious organization lies wholly or in part in this state, or by a member of the clergy residing in some other state of the United States or in the Dominion of Canada, provided he or she has first secured from the probate court of the district within which the marriage is to be solemnized a special authorization, authorizing him or her to certify the marriage if such probate judge determines that the circumstances make the special authorization desirable.

The only ministers that need to file for a permit are non-resident clergy.

Virginia

§ 20-23

When a minister of any religious denomination shall produce before the circuit court of any county or city in this Commonwealth, or before the judge of such court or before the clerk of such court at any time, proof of his ordination and of his being in regular communion with the religious society of which he is a reputed member, or proof that he holds a local minister's license and is serving as a regularly appointed pastor in his denomination, such court, or the judge thereof, or the clerk of such court at any time, may make an order authorizing such minister to celebrate the rites of matrimony in this Commonwealth. Any order made under this section may be rescinded at any time by the court or by the judge thereof.

Washington

RCW 26.04.050

The following named officers and persons, active or retired, are hereby authorized to solemnize marriages, to wit: . . . any regularly licensed or ordained minister or any priest of any church or religious denomination.

West Virginia

§48-2-402

a) Beginning the first day of September, two thousand one, the secretary of state shall, upon payment of the registration fee established by the secretary of state pursuant to subsection (d) of this section, make an order authorizing a person who is a religious representative to celebrate the rites of marriage in all the counties of the state, upon proof that the person:

(1) Is eighteen years of age or older;

(2) Is duly authorized to perform marriages by his or her church, synagogue, spiritual assembly or religious organization; and

(3) Is in regular communion with the church, synagogue, spiritual assembly or religious organization of which he or she is a member.

(b) Shall give bond in the penalty of one thousand five hundred dollars, with surety approved by the commission. Any religious representative who gives proof before the county commission of his or her ordination or authorization by his or her respective church, synagogue, spiritual assembly or religious organization is exempt from giving the bond.

§48-2-202: (a) The person solemnizing a marriage shall retain the marriage license and place an endorsement on it establishing the fact of the marriage and the time and place it was celebrated.

(b) Before the sixth day of the month after the month in which the marriage was celebrated, the person who solemnized the marriage shall forward the original of the marriage license to the clerk who issued the license.

To avoid having to provide a $1500.00 surety bond, you must present to the Secretary of State your certificate of ordination or license.

Wisconsin

765.16

(1) Any ordained member of the clergy of any religious denomination or society who continues to be an ordained member of the clergy.

Any licentiate of a denominational body or an appointee of any bishop serving as the regular member of the clergy of any church of the denomination to which the member of the clergy belongs, if not restrained from so doing by the discipline of the church or denomination.

765.17 Any member of the clergy, licentiate or appointee named in s. 765.16 who is not a resident of this state may solemnize marriages in this state if he or she possesses at the time of the marriage a letter of sponsorship from a member of the clergy of the same religious denomination or society who has a church in this state under his or her ministry.

Wyoming

20-1-106

a) Every district or circuit court judge, district court commissioner, supreme court justice, justice of the peace, magistrate and every licensed or ordained minister of the gospel, bishop, priest or rabbi, or other qualified person acting in accordance with the traditions or rites for the solemnization of marriage of any religion, denomination or religious society, may perform the ceremony of marriage in this state.

Appendix B: Wedding License Rules by U.S. State

Below are the current guidelines for each state with regards to applying for and using a Marriage License in the United States. It is important to note that these rules may be subject to change and it is wise to confirm these with the local responsible agency at reasonable intervals.

Alabama

Where do couples apply for a license?

The County Clerk's Office.

What are the age requirements?

The legal age to marry in Alabama (age of majority) is 18. Individuals ages 16 and 17 can marry in Alabama with parental consent. Both parents or legal guardians must appear with the teenager to obtain the marriage license, and provide valid identification and written consent. If the parents are divorced and one parent has full custody, he or she must bring the legal proof of divorce and full custody. If a parent has died, the teenager should provide the death certificate. Legal guardians must provide a certified copy of their court-appointed guardianship.

According to the Alabama Code Section 30 1-4, individuals under the age of 16 may not marry.

How much does a license cost?

(Can vary by county) $43.35+ for marriage license only. $63+ for license, ceremony and a certified copy. Cash or credit card requirement varies depending on County. Some locales charge $2 for using a credit card. For individuals under 18 the state also requires a $200 bond to be executed, payable to the State of Alabama.

What documents are needed?

You will need a valid Driver's License or Birth Certificate if you are over 18. All applicants must also provide a Social Security number.

If either of you are under 18, you will need a certified copy of your birth certificate. Both parents must be present with identification, or if you have a legal guardian they must be present with a court order and identification. If one or both parents are deceased, proper evidence of such must be provided.

Are there residency requirements?

You do not have to be a resident of Alabama. However, some counties may require non-residents to wait three days before being able to have a wedding ceremony performed by a county marriage official.

Is there a waiting period?

There is no waiting period in Alabama except after being divorced. Then there is a 60 day waiting period after your divorce is final.

Nonresidents who want to be married by a county official may have to wait three days. Please contact the county offices to verify whether or not you will have a waiting period.

How long is a license valid?

An Alabama marriage license is valid for 30 days.

Where is a license valid for use?

The license can only be used within the State of Alabama.

What if someone has been married previously?

If you were divorced within the last 6 months of your wedding date, you will need to show a copy of your Divorce Decree. According to Section 30-2-10 of the Alabama Code, there is a 60 day restriction on getting married after a divorce.

Are there any required tests?

No blood or medical tests are required.

Are proxy marriages allowed?

No.

Can cousins marry?

Yes.

Are common law marriages recognized?

Yes. A valid common law marriage exists in Alabama when there is a capacity to enter into a marriage, present agreement or consent t be husband and wife, public recognition of the existence of the marriage, and consummation.

Are same sex marriages legal?

Yes.

How are the documents returned?

The person performing the marriage must endorse and return the license to the clerk within 30 days after the marriage ceremony. Failure to do so is a misdemeanor.

Must the Celebrant keep records?

The Celebrant is not required to keep records of marriages.

Alaska

Where do couples apply for a license?

Vital Statistics Office or Alaska Court

What are the age requirements?

Both parties must be at least 18 years of age for a marriage license to be issued without consent from parents or legal guardians. Exception: an applicant who is under the age of 18, a member of the U.S. armed forces, and on active duty.

If either person is at least 16 years of age and under 18 years of age, they must have written consent from their legal parents. A birth certificate must be issued within 30 days of the date of the marriage license and must be submitted with the marriage application.

If either person is 14 or 15 years of age, a court order allowing the person to be married is required before the marriage license can be issued.

How much does a license cost?

The license fee is $60.00.

What documents are needed?

The Groom and Bride must present a government-issued photo ID showing their name, sex, and date of birth before a marriage license can be issued.

Are there residency requirements?

There are no residency requirements.

Is there a waiting period?

There is a 3 business day waiting period that begins once a mailed or faxed application is received by the issuing office. This means you must wait at least three full business days after the application is submitted before you can pick up the license and the marriage ceremony can be performed.

How long is a license valid?

The license is valid for 3 months from the date of issuance. The marriage must be performed before the three-month expiration or the license will no longer be valid. Refunds and extensions cannot be granted.

Where is a license valid for use?

The license is valid only for marriages performed in Alaska or in Alaska State waters.

What if someone has been married previously?

All divorces must be final and filed with the courts in the state granted. If either party has been married previously, the beginning and ending dates of all previous marriages must be listed on the application. Submitting a copy of a divorce decree is only required if the divorce or dissolution occurred less than 60 days prior to applying for the marriage license.

Are there any required tests?

No blood test or physical exam is required.

Are proxy marriages allowed?

Proxy marriages are not permitted in Alaska. The two parties must be present before two witnesses and the officiant for the ceremony to be performed.

Can cousins marry?

Yes.

Are common law marriages recognized?

No.

Are same sex marriages legal?

Yes.

How are the documents returned?

The person performing the marriage must complete two short-form certificates, and, after that person and the two witnesses have signed them, give one to each of the parties to the marriage. The original marriage certificate shall be filed as required by AS 18.50 (Vital Statistics Act) and regulations adopted under it. It must be done within 7 days.

Must the Celebrant keep records?

The Celebrant is not required to keep records of marriages.

Arizona

Where do couples apply for a license?

A Marriage License Office

What are the age requirements?

If you are 16 or 17 years old, you must have the notarized consent of your parents or legal guardian. If you are under 16, you must have the notarized consent of your parents or legal guardian as well as a court order.

How much does a license cost?

$76.00 Cash or money order.

What documents are needed?

Drivers license or identification card or other ID showing current address and date of birth. Bringing a certified copy of your birth certificate is recommended because some counties require it if you are younger than 30.

If you are 16 or 17 years old, you must have the notarized consent of your parents or legal guardian. If you are under 16, you must have the notarized consent of your parents or legal guardian as well as a court order.

Are there residency requirements?

You do not have to be a resident of Arizona.

Is there a waiting period?

There is no waiting period.

How long is a license valid?

The license is valid for 1 year.

Where is a license valid for use?

The license can only be used within the State of Arizona.

What if someone has been married previously?

Copies of the divorce decree are not required.

Are there any required tests?

No tests are required.

Are proxy marriages allowed?

No.

Can cousins marry?

Yes, first cousins may marry if both are sixty-five years of age or older. If one or both first cousins are under sixty-five years of age, they can marry if they show proof to a superior court judge that one of them is unable to reproduce.

Are common law marriages recognized?

No.

Are same sex marriages legal?

Yes.

How are the documents returned?

The person solemnizing the rites of matrimony shall endorse the act of solemnization on the license and shall return the license to the clerk within thirty days after the solemnization.

Must the Celebrant keep records?

The Celebrant is not required to keep records of marriages.

Arkansas

Where do couples apply for a license?

County Clerk's Office.

What are the age requirements?

Males and Females over 18 may apply for a marriage license on their own. Males age 17 or females ages 16 or 17 may be married with parental consent.

How much does a license cost?

Approximately $58+ (determined by county). Cash only. No checks accepted. No refunds.

What documents are needed?

Males and females 21 or under must present a state-certified copy of their birth certificates or an active Military Identification Card or valid passport.

Note: No witnesses are required in Arkansas.

Males and females 21 or older may present a valid driver's license showing their correct name and date of birth or any documents listed above.

If your name has changed through a divorce and your driver's license does not reflect this change, you will need to bring a certified copy of your divorce decree.

Are there residency requirements?

No.

Is there a waiting period?

The license may be used immediately.

How long is a license valid?

Marriage licenses are valid for 60 days. License must be returned, used or unused, within 60 days for recording or a $100 bond will be executed against all applicants for license.

Where is a license valid for use?

The license may be used anywhere in the state of Arkansas, but must be returned to the County Clerk's Office where you first applied.

What if someone has been married previously?

If your name has changed through a divorce and your driver's license does not reflect this change, you will need to bring a certified copy of your divorce decree. There is no waiting period required on Arkansas after a divorce is final.

Are there any required tests?

No.

Are proxy marriages allowed?

No.

Can cousins marry?

No.

Are common law marriages recognized?

No.

Are same sex marriages legal?

Yes.

How are the documents returned?

The marriage license must be completed by the minister and returned to the county clerk within 60 days from the date the license was issued.

Must the Celebrant keep records?

The Celebrant is not required to keep records of marriages.

California

Where do couples apply for a license?

The County Clerk's Office.

What are the age requirements?

California is one of just a few states lacking a minimum age for marriage. However, minors (under the age of 18) must obtain both parental consent and a court order before they may legally tie the knot. Although couples seldom get married before they reach the age of majority, it is made available primarily to allow pregnant minors to marry.

How much does a license cost?

The fee for a marriage license in California varies from county to county. It will cost you between $35.00+ and $100.00+ to get married in California. Some California counties will only accept cash. Please call ahead to verify whether or not you need cash.

What documents are needed?

Both parties must appear in person and bring valid picture identification to the County Clerk's Office. Valid picture identification is one that contains a photograph, date of birth, and an issue and expiration date, such as a state issued identification card, drivers license, passport, military identification, etc. Some counties may also require a copy of your birth certificate.

Are there residency requirements?

You do not need to be a California resident to marry in California.

Is there a waiting period?

No.

How long is a license valid?

Marriage licenses are valid for 90 days from the date of issuance. If you do not get married within 90 days, you must purchase a new license.

Where is a license valid for use?

The license is valid anywhere in California

What if someone has been married previously?

If you have been married before, you will need to know the specific date your last marriage ended, and how it ended (death, Dissolution, Divorce or Nullity). Some counties may require a copy of the final judgment if your previous marriage ended by dissolution or nullity.

Are there any required tests?

No tests required.

Are proxy marriages allowed?

No.

Can cousins marry?

Yes.

Are common law marriages recognized?

No.

Are same sex marriages legal?

Yes.

How are the documents returned?

Ministers must complete the marriage license and return it to the county clerk within 4 days after the marriage.

Must the Celebrant keep records?

The Celebrant is not required to keep records of marriages.

Colorado

Where do couples apply for a license?

County Clerk's Office.

What are the age requirements?

If you are 16 or 17, in Colorado you will need consent of both parents (or parent having legal custody), or guardian, or seek judicial approval. If you are under 16, a Judicial Court Order along with parental consent is necessary.

How much does a license cost?

Marriage license is $30. Cash only. No Credit Cards or Checks accepted.

What documents are needed?

In Colorado, you will need to bring government issued ID such as your driver's license, visa, passport, state or military ID. Bring your social security cards.

Are there residency requirements?

No.

Is there a waiting period?

No.

How long is a license valid?

License is valid for 30 days.

Where is a license valid for use?

License is valid in Colorado.

What if someone has been married previously?

Divorced persons must provide the approximate date of divorce and a location where the decree was issued. If the divorce occurred within 90 days of the request for a marriage license, a copy of the decree must also be present.

Are there any required tests?

No.

Are proxy marriages allowed?

Marriage by proxy is allowed in Colorado only if either the groom or bride cannot appear due to illness, is out of the state of Colorado, or incarcerated.

In these cases, the bride or groom can obtain an absentee application. It must be notarized. Identification for the absent party must be provided by the other soon to be spouse when applying for the license

Can cousins marry?

Yes.

Are common law marriages recognized?

Yes

Are same sex marriages legal?

Yes.

How are the documents returned?

Ministers must send a marriage certificate to the county clerk.

Must the Celebrant keep records?

The Celebrant is not required to keep records of marriages.

Connecticut

Where do couples apply for a license?

The Town Clerk's Office. Although you do not have to be a resident of Connecticut, you do need to apply in either the town where one of you lives, or in the town where you plan on getting married.

If it is difficult for you both to appear at the same time at the Clerk's office to apply for your marriage license, you can appear individually.

What are the age requirements?

If under 18 years of age, parental consent is needed. If under 16 years of age, the written consent of the judge of probate for the district where the minor resides must be obtained.

How much does a license cost?

The fee is $30. Most locales won't accept credit cards or out-of-state checks. Cash is best.

What documents are needed?

Connecticut law requires that you present photo ID such as a driver's license or a passport. You also need to know the following:

1. Your social security numbers.

2. Your mother's maiden name.

3. Your parent's birthplaces.

4. Date and location of your wedding.

5. Name and contact info of your wedding officiant.

Are there residency requirements?

Although you do not have to be a resident of Connecticut, you do need to apply in either the town where one of you lives, or in the town where you plan on getting married.

Is there a waiting period?

No. Some towns may require you to pick the license up the next day.

How long is a license valid?

A marriage license in Connecticut is valid for 65 days.

Where is a license valid for use?

A marriage license in Connecticut is only valid in Connecticut.

What if someone has been married previously?

You will need to show your divorce decree, or have information regarding date, county and state of death of previous spouse. If your name has changed, you need to bring a certified copy of your divorce decree.

Are there any required tests?

No.

Are proxy marriages allowed?

No.

Can cousins marry?

Yes.

Are common law marriages recognized?

No.

Are same sex marriages legal?

Yes.

How are the documents returned?

Marriage license must be completed by the minister and returned to the city or town clerk.

Must the Celebrant keep records?

The Celebrant is not required to keep records of marriages.

Delaware

Where do couples apply for a license?

Clerk of the Peace

What are the age requirements?

You must be at least 18 years of age to marry without authorization. Minors must petition Family Court for authorization to marry.

How much does a license cost?

$50.00 if either applicant is a Delaware resident. $100.00 if neither applicant is a Delaware resident.

What documents are needed?

The couple must apply together in person.

A valid state ID or Diver's License issued by the DMV, Passport, U.S. Visa I.D. Card, Federal Driver's License, Military I.D. or Government Consulate I.D. is required to apply for a marriage license.

To verify the authenticity of an applicant's identification, the office of the Clerk of the Peace may also require additional documentation such as birth certificate or social security card.

Special authorization is required if either party is on probation or parole.

Are there residency requirements?

No.

Is there a waiting period?

Persons intending to be married in Delaware shall obtain a marriage license at least 24 hours prior to the time of the ceremony. This applies to residents as well as non-residents.

How long is a license valid?

Marriage licenses are valid for 30 days.

Where is a license valid for use?

Marriage licenses are only valid in Delaware.

What if someone has been married previously?

If individuals have previously been married, an original or certified copy of the Divorce Decree, Annulment, or Death Certificate is required.

Are there any required tests?

No.

Are proxy marriages allowed?

No.

Can cousins marry?

No.

Are common law marriages recognized?

No.

Are same sex marriages legal?

Yes.

Note: Ministers do not need to be licensed to perform marriages but they must report their name and address to the local registrar in the district in which they live. Ministers must keep a copy of the marriage license for at least one year. Also, the minister must, within 4 days, complete and return forms required by the State Board of Health to the Clerk of the Peace.

Neither Bride or Groom may be married under the influence of alcohol.

How are the documents returned?

The minister must, within 4 days, complete and return forms required by the State Board of Health to the clerk of the peace.

Must the Celebrant keep records?

Ministers must keep the marriage license or a copy for at least one year.

District of Columbia

Where do couples apply for a license?

Moultrie Courthouse

500 Indiana Avenue, N.W.

Room 4485

Washington, DC 20001

(202) 879 4840

8:30 AM – 5:00 PM M-F

What are the age requirements?

If 16 or 17 years of age consent of the parent or guardian is required. Proof of age for the applicants must be shown at the time of application and may be demonstrated by drivers licenses, birth certificates, passports, or similar official documents.

How much does a license cost?

$45 (Cash or Money Order). Note: $35 portion of the fee may be waived for couples who are registered in the District as domestic partners. These couples should bring their proof of registration and $10 license fee.

What documents are needed?

A completed application form.

Proof of age.

Note: You must include the name of the officiant performing the wedding ceremony on your application. Your officiant must be authorized by the Court and registered by the Marriage Bureau to legally perform ceremonies in the District of Columbia.

Are there residency requirements?

No.

Is there a waiting period?

3 full business days must pass between the day of application and the day that the license can be issued. In addition, there may be a processing delay. Confirm your day of pickup when you apply.

How long is a license valid?

No expiration date.

Where is a license valid for use?

The District of Columbia.

What if someone has been married previously?

If you were previously married, the date of your divorce or the date of your spouse's death must be provided. Bring a certified copy of the divorce decree or death certificate. If necessary, a copy of your divorce records or spouse's death certificate can be ordered from your local vital records office and mailed to you.

Are there any required tests?

Yes, the couple is required to take a blood test for syphilis prior to receiving a license. The bride is also required to take a blood test for venereal disease. The blood test must be analyzed by a state certified laboratory and recorded on a state form. This form can be obtained from the physician, clinic, or the Office of the Town Clerk. Test results become invalid after 30 days.

Are proxy marriages allowed?

No.

Can cousins marry?

Yes, cousin marriages (first, second, etc) are allowed to take place.

Are common law marriages recognized?

Yes.

Are same sex marriages legal?

Yes.

How are the documents returned?

Marriage licenses are addressed to the minister who will perform the ceremony. The minister must complete a marriage certificate for the bride and for the groom and return another certificate to the clerk of the District of Columbia Court of General Sessions within 10 days after the marriage.

Must the Celebrant keep records?

The Celebrant is not required to keep records of marriages.

Florida

Where do couples apply for a license?

County Clerk's Office

What are the age requirements?

If an individual is under 18 years of age, but older than 16 years of age, a marriage license can be obtained with parental consent. If a parent has sole custody or the other parent is dead, the permission of one parent is sufficient if proof of custody is supplied. If a person is under the age of 16, the marriage license has to be issued by a county judge, with or without parental permission. If a minor's parents are both deceased and there is not an appointed guardian, he / she may apply for a marriage license and produce death certificates for both parents. A minor who has previously married may apply for a license. A minor who swears that they have a child or are expecting a baby, can apply for a license if the pregnancy has been verified by a written statement from a licensed physician. A county court judge may at his / her discretion issue or not issue a license for them to marry.

How much does a license cost?

$93.50. Marriage license fees can be reduced by up to $32.50 if you complete a licensed Florida pre-marital course. Many locales do accept credit cards now, but be sure to check with the local county recorder or clerk to make sure. Here credit cards are accepted an extra charge may be required.

What documents are needed?

Florida requires that you have a picture ID such as a driver's license and your Social Security card or a valid passport or I-94 card. You may be asked for a certified copy of your birth certificate. You will need a copy of your birth certificate if under 18 years of age.

Are there residency requirements?

No.

Is there a waiting period?

There is no waiting period for Florida residents who have completed a state sanctioned marriage preparation course within the last 12 months. There is a three-day waiting period for Florida residents who have not taken the course. Court Clerks are allowed to waive the three-day waiting period in the event of a "hardship" case.

How long is a license valid?

License is valid for 60 days.

Where is a license valid for use?

Anywhere in Florida.

What if someone has been married previously?

If you have been previously married, the date of your divorce or date of your spouse's death must be supplied. If the divorce or spouse's death occurred within the past 30 days, a certified copy of the divorce decree or death certificate is required.

Are there any required tests?

No.

Are proxy marriages allowed?

No.?

Can cousins marry?

Yes.?

Are common law marriages recognized?

No.

Are same sex marriages legal?

Yes.

How are the documents returned?

Ministers must complete a certificate of marriage on the marriage license and return it to the office from which it was issued.

Must the Celebrant keep records?

The Celebrant is not required to keep records of marriages.

Note: Effective January 1999 Florida couples have to consider the consequences of divorce before they can get married. Prospective brides and grooms are now required to read a small booklet which describes situations such as how a court would divide their assets and information about child support payments. The good side of all this is that licenses are available at a reduced price if a couple attends a four-hour course to improve communication, financial and parenting skills before marriage.

Georgia

Where do couples apply for a license?

The County Probate Court.

What are the age requirements?

You must be at least 16 years of age in order to obtain a license in Georgia. If you are 16 or 17 years of age, both parents and legal guardians must give their consent in person unless his / her rights have been terminated by an Order of a court (in which case the order must be presented).

How much does a license cost?

It costs approximately $65.00 + to get married in Georgia. Most counties will only accept cash. The amount of the marriage license fee will be decreased by showing proof of receiving premarital counseling.

Note: Premarital Education:

Under Georgia Law, a man and woman who present to the court at the time of making application a certificate of completion of a qualifying premarital education program shall not be assessed a full marriage license fee. The premarital education shall include at least six hours of instruction involving marital issues, which may include but not be limited to conflict management, communication skills, financial responsibilities, child and parenting responsibilities, and extended family roles. The premarital education shall be completed within 12 months prior to the application for a marriage license and the couple shall undergo the premarital education together. The premarital education shall be performed by:

(1) A professional counselor, social worker, or marriage and family therapist who is licensed pursuant to Chapter 10A of Title 43;

(2) A psychiatrist who is licensed as a physician pursuant to Chapter 34 of Title 43;

(3) A psychologist who is licensed pursuant to Chapter 39 of Title 43; or

(4) An active member of the clergy when in the course of his or her service as clergy or his or her designee, including retired clergy, provided that a designee is trained and skilled in premarital education.

Cobb County offers a free Marital Workshop called Focus On Forever. It is a skill-based non-religious workshop designed to address issues concerning communication and listening skills, anger management, and financial planning. Contact the Cobb County Superior Court for more information.

By state law, counties in Georgia now charge more for a marriage license if you do not show certification of a premarital education program.

What documents are needed?

Two valid forms of ID such as driver's license, birth certificate, U.S. passport, Armed Forces ID card, or Resident Alien ID card. Applicants will also be asked to fill out a brief form.

Note: The applicants must designate on the application the legal surname that will be used after the marriage. An applicant may choose his or her given surname or his or her surname as changed by order of the superior court, the surname from a previous marriage, the spouse's surname, or a combination of the spouse's surname and the applicant's given or changed surname from a previous marriage.

Are there residency requirements?

No.

Note: If one of the parties is a resident of Georgia, the license can be issued in any county.

If neither party is a resident of Georgia, the license must be issued in the county in which the marriage ceremony is to be performed.

Is there a waiting period?

No.

How long is a license valid?

Your marriage license will never expire once it's been issued. However, some counties prefer the license to be used within six months.

Where is a license valid for use?

A Georgia marriage license is valid state wide.

What if someone has been married previously?

If divorced, however long ago, you will need to show a copy of your divorce decree.

You can obtain a copy of your final divorce decree from the Superior Court in the county in which you filed for divorce.

Are there any required tests?

No.

Are proxy marriages allowed?

No.

Can cousins marry?

Yes. First cousins may marry.

Are common law marriages recognized?

If before 1987 your common law marriage is recognized with documentation. Otherwise, common law marriage is not recognized.

Are same sex marriages legal?

No.

How are the documents returned?

Ministers must complete a certificate of marriage and return it within 30 days after the marriage.

Must the Celebrant keep records?

The Celebrant is not required to keep records of marriages.

Hawaii

Where do couples apply for a license?

Marriage License Office.

What are the age requirements?

You must be at least 18 years of age or older to marry without parental consent. A birth certificate may be necessary to show proof of age.

If either partner is under 18, parental consent forms must be signed. You will need a certified copy of your birth certificate. If you are under 16 you cannot marry without a court order. In the case of pregnancy parental consent is still required or consent of the judge of family court.

How much does a license cost?

$65.($5 of which is processing fee) Cash only. For this they get one certificate mailed. Each extra is $10.

What documents are needed?

Two valid forms of ID such as a driver's license, birth certificate, U.S. passport, Armed Forces ID card, or Resident Alien ID card. Applicants will also be asked to fill out a Marriage License Application Form.

Both the bride and groom must prepare an official application and file the application in person with the marriage license agent. The application will not be accepted if sent by either postal mail or e-mail.

Note:

Arrange for a licensed minister, or a marriage performer, to conduct your wedding ceremony. If you do not have a marriage officiant, call the Hawaii Visitors and Convention Bureau at (808) 924-0266 for a list of persons licensed to perform weddings in Hawaii.

Ministers must obtain a license from the department of health before performing marriages. Ministers must keep a record of all marriages they perform.

Ministers must report all marriages they perform to the department of health.

Are there residency requirements?

No.

Is there a waiting period?

No.

How long is a license valid?

30 days.

Where is a license valid for use?

Only within Hawaii.

What if someone has been married previously?

If previously married, the date of divorce or date of spouse's death must be provided.

Are there any required tests?

No.

Are proxy marriages allowed?

No.

Can cousins marry?

Cousins may marry. However, the blood relationship between the prospective bride and groom cannot be closer than first cousins.

Are common law marriages recognized?

No.

Are same sex marriages legal?

Yes.

How are the documents returned?

Ministers must obtain a license from the department of health before performing marriages. Ministers must report all marriages they perform to the department of health.

Must the Celebrant keep records?

Ministers must keep a record of all marriages they perform. Keep in a record book and copies of the documents.

Idaho

Where do couples apply for a license?

The County Clerk or Recorder. These offices, some of which are referred to as the "marriage license bureau," are usually located in the county probate court or circuit court.

What are the age requirements?

Both parties age 18 or older – no consent requirements.

Between 16 and 17 – Applicants must present one of the following:

 - Original Birth Certificate or Certified Copy

 - Current Driver's License

 - Passport

Under 16 years – Applicants must present a Court Order

How much does a license cost?

$30. Cash Only.

What documents are needed?

Valid Driver's License and Birth Certificate.

Are there residency requirements?

No.

Is there a waiting period?

No.

How long is a license valid?

There is no expiration on the license. It remains good as long as the same two parties listed use it.

Where is a license valid for use?

Only in Idaho.

What if someone has been married previously?

If previously married, the date of divorce or date of spouse's death must be provided.

Are there any required tests?

No blood tests. Idaho Code 32-412A requires both parties to read and sign a premarital AIDS educational pamphlet.

Are proxy marriages allowed?

No.

Can cousins marry?

No.

Are common law marriages recognized?

Yes.

Are same sex marriages legal?

Yes.

How are the documents returned?

Ministers must give a marriage certificate to the bride and to the groom. Also, the minister must complete the license and marriage certificate and return it to the recorder who issued it within 30 days after the marriage.

Must the Celebrant keep records?

The Celebrant is not required to keep records of marriages.

Illinois

Where do couples apply for a license?

County Clerk Office

What are the age requirements?

People older than 18 years of age who are not blood relatives may marry without parental consent.

Applicants between the ages of 16 and 17 may obtain a marriage license by presenting the following information:

- Sworn consent from each parent, each legal guardian or a judge – in person – before the county clerk at the time of the application. Those giving consent must provide proper identification, including a: valid driver's license; valid state identification card; valid Illinois Department of Public Aid card; valid passport. (If the legal guardian is giving consent, a certified copy of the guardianship papers must be provided.)

How much does a license cost?

$30 (though some counties mat charge $60. The cost of receiving a marriage license varies from county to county and some Illinois counties will only accept cash.

What documents are needed?

Any of the following documents will be accepted:

- Valid U.S. Driver's License
- Valid U.S. state identification card
- Valid U.S. passport, Valid U.S. military identification card,
- Valid Illinois Department of Public Aid card (the I.D. and the medical card).

If you do not have any of the above forms of identification, then you MUST present TWO (2) of the following pieces of identification:

- A certified copy of a birth certificate.
- A valid U.S. resident alien card.
- U.S. naturalization papers.
- A valid foreign passport.
- All consulate identification cards. Affidavits are not acceptable.
- A baptismal record (the date of birth of the applicant must appear on this record).
- A life insurance policy, which has been in effect for one (1) year (the applicant's date of birth must appear on the document).
- A certified copy of their birth certificate.
- A second piece of identification showing date of birth.
- At least one parent of any applicant under the age of 18 must be present.

Are there residency requirements?

No. However, non-residents cannot obtain a marriage license if said marriage would be void in their state.

Is there a waiting period?

No.

How long is a license valid?

60 Days.

Where is a license valid for use?

License is valid only in the county in which it was issued.

What if someone has been married previously?

If either applicant is divorced, they must provide final divorce papers signed by the judge.

If you were previously married, the date of your divorce or the date of your spouse's death must be provided. If the divorce or spouse's death had taken place within the last 6 months, bring a certified copy of the divorce decree or death certificate. If necessary, a copy of your divorce records or spouse's death certificate can be ordered from your local vital records office and mailed to you.

Are there any required tests?

No.

Are proxy marriages allowed?

No

Can cousins marry?

First cousins older than the age of 50 may marry.

Are common law marriages recognized?

No.

Are same sex marriages legal?

Yes.

How are the documents returned?

Either the person solemnizing the marriage, or, if no individual acting alone solemnized the marriage, both parties to the marriage, shall complete the marriage certificate form and forward it to the county clerk within 10 days after such marriage is solemnized.

Must the Celebrant keep records?

The Celebrant is not required to keep records of marriages.

Indiana

Where do couples apply for a license?

The County Clerk's Office where one of the couple resides, or for non-residents in the county where the marriage will be solemnized.

What are the age requirements?

If both applicants are 18 or over a license can be issued without consent.

If one or both applicants are 17, parents or legal guardians must be present to provide consent.

If one or both applicants are younger than 17 they must have a court order granting permission for the marriage license.

How much does a license cost?

Indiana's marriage license application fee is $18 if one or both parties are Indiana residents and $60.00 for out-of-state residents.

Some offices also charge an additional document fee of $2.00. Each copy of the Certified Marriage License (required for name change at BMV, SSN, etc.) is also $2.00.

Most counties require these fees to be paid in cash.

What documents are needed?

You will need any one of the following forms of identification to prove your identity and date of birth:

- Current, valid driver's license or state issued ID card.

- Passport

- Birth Certificate

You will also be required to provide your Social Security Number, although your Social Security Card may not be required.

The Clerk's Office will collect some family information from you that will be reported to the Indiana State Library for the purposes of genealogical research. You will need to provide the following for both parents:

- Full Name

- Last known address

- Birthplace (state or foreign country)

Are there residency requirements?

No.

Is there a waiting period?

No.

How long is a license valid?

60 Days.

Where is a license valid for use?

Only in the State of Indiana.

What if someone has been married previously?

You will need to know how the marriages ended (death, divorce, annulment) and the month and year the marriages ended. A few counties require a copy of the divorce decree if divorced within the last two years.

Are there any required tests?

No.

Are proxy marriages allowed?

No.

Can cousins marry?

Applicants cannot marry if they are more closely related than second cousins (though there is an exception if you are first cousins and both are at least 65 years of age).

Are common law marriages recognized?

No.

Are same sex marriages legal?

Yes.

How are the documents returned?

Ministers must return the marriage license and a certificate of marriage to the clerk of the circuit court within 3 months after the marriage.

Must the Celebrant keep records?

The Celebrant is not required to keep records of marriages.

Iowa

Where do couples apply for a license?

County Clerk's Office

What are the age requirements?

Applicants 16 or 17 years of age need to have parental consent.

How much does a license cost?

The marriage license fee is roughly $35.00 dollars, although fees may vary from county to county. Accepted forms of payment are cash.

What documents are needed?

Picture identification is required. You also need to provide Social Security information.

Note: You need to have one witness (over 18 years of age) with you when you apply for the license.

Are there residency requirements?

No.

Is there a waiting period?

Yes. There is a waiting period of 3 business days.

How long is a license valid?

6 months.

Where is a license valid for use?

In the state of Iowa.

What if someone has been married previously?

If previously married, the date of divorce or date of spouse's death must be provided.

Are there any required tests?

No.

Are proxy marriages allowed?

No. However, if one of you can't be present at the Recorder's Office to apply for the license, the absent party can sign the Iowa marriage license application before a Notary Public.

Can cousins marry?

No.

Are common law marriages recognized?

Yes.

Are same sex marriages legal?

Yes.

How are the documents returned?

The minister must report the marriage to the clerk of the district court within 15 days after the marriage.

Must the Celebrant keep records?

The Celebrant is not required to keep records of marriages.

Kansas

Where do couples apply for a license?

Clerk of the District Court.

What are the age requirements?

Any applicant who is under 18 must have either:

- Notarized, written consent of all then living parents and legal guardians OR

- Notarized, written consent of one parent or legal guardian and consent of a district court judge.

How much does a license cost?

$85.50. Cash is required in most counties. Money orders are accepted in some counties and should be payable to "Clerk of the District Court". The money is non-refundable.

What documents are needed?

A certified Birth Certificate.

Full name (First, Middle and Last)

Residence (City, county and state)

Birthplace (State or foreign country)

Date of Birth

Race

Highest level of education completed

Both applicants fathers' full name (First, Middle and Last)

Both applicants mothers' full name (First, Middle and Maiden)

All birthplaces (State or foreign country)

Name and address of person performing ceremony, if known.

Are there residency requirements?

No.

Is there a waiting period?

There is a 3 day waiting period, after the application is made, before you may pick up the license.

How long is a license valid?

6 months.

Where is a license valid for use?

In the State of Kansas.

What if someone has been married previously?

If previously married, how last marriage ended and when. Number of this marriage.

Are there any required tests?

No.

Are proxy marriages allowed?

No.

Can cousins marry?

No.

Are common law marriages recognized?

Yes.

Are same sex marriages legal?

Yes.

How are the documents returned?

The Minister must return the marriage license and a certificate of marriage to the probate judge who issued the marriage license within 10 days after the marriage.

Must the Celebrant keep records?

The Celebrant is not required to keep records of marriages.

Kentucky

Where do couples apply for a license?

The County Clerk

What are the age requirements?

You must be at least 18 years of age or older to marry without parental consent. A birth certificate may be necessary to show proof of age.

If either partner is under 18, parental consent forms must be signed. You will need a certified copy of your birth certificate. If you are under 16 you cannot marry without a court order. A minor who is pregnant does not need parental consent as long as the pregnancy is verified in a written statement by a licensed physician. Minors cannot marry if parents or guardians are not residents of the state.

How much does a license cost?

$35.50 - $37.00) Fees vary from county to county. Cash, certified check, cashier's check, or money order only.

What documents are needed?

Acceptable forms of ID in accordance with the statute and recorders manual include: Drivers License, current picture ID, Social Security Card, birth certificate, or passport.

Are there residency requirements?

No.

Is there a waiting period?

No.

How long is a license valid?

30 Days.

Where is a license valid for use?

In the State of Kentucky.

What if someone has been married previously?

If previously married, the date of divorce or date of spouse's death must be provided.

Are there any required tests?

No.

Are proxy marriages allowed?

No.

Can cousins marry?

No.

Are common law marriages recognized?

No.

Are same sex marriages legal?

No.

How are the documents returned?

Ministers must return the marriage license and marriage certificate to the county clerk within 3 months after the marriage.

Must the Celebrant keep records?

The Celebrant is not required to keep records of marriages.

Louisiana

Where do couples apply for a license?

Parish Clerk of Court

What are the age requirements?

Applicants under 18 years of age must also bring:

 - Both parents to sign consent forms. Both parents must bring their drivers license.

 - If one parent has full custody, that parent must come in to sign consent forms with his / her driver's license and custody papers showing full custody. Joint custody requires both parent's consent.

How much does a license cost?

$25 - $32. The cost varies from parish to parish and some will only accept cash.

What documents are needed?

A certified copy of each party's birth certificate or birth card. If either party was born out-of-country, a translated notarized birth certificate along with a valid state ID card or driver's license must be presented.

Each party must have proof of their social security number.

If either party was born outside the United States their must present a valid passport or naturalization certificate or residency card.

Plus: Address for bride and groom and whether such is within city limits, father's and mother's full name plus maiden name and the state in which each was born, and the highest grade of education completed by the bride and groom.

Are there residency requirements?

No.

Is there a waiting period?

72 hours between issuance of the license and the ceremony. The waiting period can be waived by a district judge or justice of the peace in the parish where the license was issued.

How long is a license valid?

30 days.

Where is a license valid for use?

Any parish in Louisiana.

What if someone has been married previously?

If either party is divorced, he / she must present a certified copy of the final divorce decree.

If either party is widowed, he / she must present a certified copy of a death certificate.

Are there any required tests?

No.

Are proxy marriages allowed?

No.

Can cousins marry?

No.

Are common law marriages recognized?

No.

Are same sex marriages legal?

No.

How are the documents returned?

After performing a marriage, the minister must complete a marriage certificate and return it to the clerk of the district court.

Must the Celebrant keep records?

The Celebrant is not required to keep records of marriages.

Maine

Where do couples apply for a license?

Town Clerk / Town Office

If both of you are residents of the state of Maine, you must both apply in the town where the Maine resident holds residency. If you are residents of different Maine towns, you both may apply in one town or the other – you do not need to apply separately in each town.

If one is from out of state, then both of you should apply in the town where one holds residency.

If neither of you is resident in Maine, then you may apply in any Maine town Office. It need not be the same town where you plan to be married.

What are the age requirements?

Applicants must be over 18 years old. Written parental consent is required for an applicant under 18. Written parental consent and written consent of a judge are required for an applicant under 16.

How much does a license cost?

$40

What documents are needed?

Photo ID and a driver's license.

Are there residency requirements?

No.

Is there a waiting period?

No.

How long is a license valid?

90 Days.

Where is a license valid for use?

The State of Maine.

What if someone has been married previously?

If this is not the first marriage for one of you, bring a certified copy (raised seal) of the divorce from or death certificate of the last spouse.

Are there any required tests?

No.

Are proxy marriages allowed?

No.

Can cousins marry?

No. (First cousins must have Pre-marital counseling).

Are common law marriages recognized?

No.

Are same sex marriages legal?

Yes.

How are the documents returned?

After the marriage, the minister must file a copy of the record of marriage with the town clerk where the license was issued. The license must be returned within 7 days.

Must the Celebrant keep records?

The Celebrant is not required to keep records of marriages.

Maryland

Where do couples apply for a license?

The local Clerk of the Court

What are the age requirements?

If under 18 parental consent is required. If between 16 and 18 years of age, one of your parents or a guardian must be with you and provide written consent.

If under 16 years of age, you will need both the written consent of your custodial parent or guardian and the written approval of a judge of the Orphans' Court Division of the Court of Common Pleas.

If you are under 18, pregnant or have a child, and show certificate from a licensed physician stating you are pregnant or have had a child, the parental consent requirement may be waived.

How much does a license cost?

Between $35 and $85.The charge varies from city to county.

If you have completed a state recognized pre-marital preparation course, you may receive a discount on the license fee.

What documents are needed?

Photo ID and Social Security number. A birth certificate may be necessary to prove your age.

However, a non-resident form may be applied for by non-US residents. This form must be certified by the equivalent official in your country of residence.

Are there residency requirements?

No.

Is there a waiting period?

There is a waiting period of 48 hours in Maryland to get married. You receive the license on application but it does not become valid for 48 hours.

How long is a license valid?

6 Months

Where is a license valid for use?

You must be married in the county where you purchased your license.

What if someone has been married previously?

Maryland requires you have information regarding date, county and state of death of your previous spouse.

Are there any required tests?

No.

Are proxy marriages allowed?

No.

Can cousins marry?

Yes. First cousins may marry.

Are common law marriages recognized?

No.

Are same sex marriages legal?

Yes.

How are the documents returned?

The Minister must complete the marriage license and marriage certificate and give one certificate to the couple. The official certification must be returned to the clerk of the court offices within five days after the marriage.

Must the Celebrant keep records?

The Celebrant is not required to keep records of marriages.

Massachusetts

Where do couples apply for a license?

City or Town Clerk

What are the age requirements?

Parental consent is needed if under 18 years of age. If you are between 16-18 years of age, one of your parents or guardian must be with you and provide written consent.

If you are under 16 years of age, you will need both the written consent of your custodial parent or guardian and the written approval of a judge of the Orphans' Court Division of the Court of Common Pleas.

If you are under 18, pregnant or have had a child, and show a certificate from a licensed physician stating you are pregnant or have had a child, the parental consent requirement may be waived.

How much does a license cost?

The fee for filing the Intention of Marriage varies from town to town. The state statute stipulates a fee of $4 for the license but it allows cities and towns by a vote of their city councils, boards of selectmen or town meeting, or by a change in the by-laws, to set their own fee.

What documents are needed?

Picture ID such as driver's license. You should know your Social security numbers.

Are there residency requirements?

No.

Is there a waiting period?

3 days. Sundays and holidays are included in the three days, but the day the application is made is not. For example, if you apply on Friday, your license will be issued on or after Monday. Check with your town clerk to determine whether you must pick it up in person, or if it can be mailed.

How long is a license valid?

60 Days.

Where is a license valid for use?

Within the Commonwealth of Massachusetts.

What if someone has been married previously?

You are not required to present a divorce certificate when filing intentions to marry. However, it is extremely important that an individual who has been divorced be certain that his/her divorce is absolute. If you are uncertain as to the absolute date of your divorce, you should contact the court where the divorce was granted. In Massachusetts, a divorce does not become absolute until 90 days after the divorce nisi has been granted, regardless of the grounds for divorce.

Are there any required tests?

No.

Are proxy marriages allowed?

No.

Can cousins marry?

Yes.

Are common law marriages recognized?

No.

Are same sex marriages legal?

Yes.

How are the documents returned?

Ministers must return a certificate of the marriage to the town clerk or registrar who issued the marriage license and to the town clerk of the town where the marriage was performed.

Must the Celebrant keep records?

Ministers must keep records of all marriages they perform.

Michigan

Where do couples apply for a license?

County Register of Deeds.

Residents need to apply for their marriage license in the county in which one of them lives. Non-residents need to apply for their marriage license in the county where they plan on getting married.

Even though you apply for your marriage license in the county you live in you can get married any place in the state.

What are the age requirements?

If you are 16 or 17 years old, you can get married with parental consent. Your parents must appear with their own identification and if a custodial parent, proof of their custody. If you are 15 or younger, you will need both parental consent and the approval of the probate court.

How much does a license cost?

$20 if you are a resident of Michigan. $30 for non-residents. Some counties may charge more. Bring cash. Most counties do not accept checks.

What documents are needed?

Picture ID such as Drivers License. You can also use Military ID. You must also have a certified copy of your birth certificates.

You will need to know your parents addresses, and your mothers' maiden names. Foreign birth certificates need to be translated into English, and be notarized.

Are there residency requirements?

No.

Is there a waiting period?

There is a mandatory 3 day waiting period before your license is issued to you. In most states, the waiting period does not include Saturdays, Sundays or federal holidays. In some instances, the day the application is filed is not included within the waiting period timeline.

How long is a license valid?

33 Days.

Where is a license valid for use?

Anywhere in the State of Michigan.

What if someone has been married previously?

You need to know the date (mm/dd/yy) and how the last marriage ended. If it was within the last 6 months, you will need to bring proof of the divorce that can be left with the Clerk.

Are there any required tests?

No.

Are proxy marriages allowed?

No. However, only one of you need to be present and have all required documentation when applying for a marriage license. You will need to show a photocopy of the front and back of your partner's driver's license.

Can cousins marry?

No.

Are common law marriages recognized?

No.

Are same sex marriages legal?

No.

How are the documents returned?

Ministers must complete a marriage certificate and give one to the couple. Another marriage certificate must be returned to the county clerk who issued the license within 10 days after the marriage.

Must the Celebrant keep records?

The Celebrant is not required to keep records of marriages.

Minnesota

Where do couples apply for a license?

The County Recorder.

What are the age requirements?

Applicants must be 18 years of age to obtain a license without parental consent.

If either partner is under 18, parental consent forms must be signed. You will need a certified copy of your birth certificate. If you are under 16 you cannot marry without a court order.

How much does a license cost?

The marriage license fee is $40.00 for parties who have completed at least 12 hours of premarital education (see requirements below). The fee for the license is $115.00 if you have not met the premarital education requirements.

Reduced Fee Requirements: In order to qualify for the reduced fee, the parties must submit a signed and dated statement from the person who provided the premarital education confirming that it was received. The premarital education must be provided by a licensed or ordained minister or the minister's designee, a person authorized to solemnize marriages under Minnesota Statutes, section 517.18, or a person authorized to practice marriage and family therapy under Minnesota Statutes, section 148B.33. The education must include the use of premarital inventory and the teaching of communication and conflict management skills.

The statement from the person who provided the premarital education must have the the following wording on their business letterhead stationery, signed and notarized or under church seal or follow the format found in Minnesota Statutes, section 517.08 subd 1b:

I, (name of educator), confirm that (full legal name of both parties) received at least 12 hours of premarital education that included the use of a premarital inventory and the teaching of communication and conflict management skills. I am a licensed or ordained minister, a person authorized to solemnize marriages under Minnesota Statutes, section 517.18, or a person authorized to practice marriage and family therapy under Minnesota Statutes, section 148B.33.

The names of the parties in the educator's statement must be identical to the legal names of the parties as they appear in the marriage license application. This document must be clear and legible and on 8 1/2 X 11 paper.

What documents are needed?

A valid photo ID and proof of your Social Security number. You may also need to bring a copy of your birth certificate.

You must provide after-marriage names and addresses.

Are there residency requirements?

No.

Is there a waiting period?

5 days between applying for and receiving your license.

How long is a license valid?

6 Months.

Where is a license valid for use?

The State of Minnesota.

What if someone has been married previously?

If previously married and now divorced, you must bring the divorce decree with you.

Are there any required tests?

No.

Are proxy marriages allowed?

No.

Can cousins marry?

No.

Are common law marriages recognized?

No. However, the state does recognize common law marriages that are valid in other states.

Are same sex marriages legal?

Yes.

How are the documents returned?

Ministers must give a marriage certificate to the bride and groom and also file a certificate with the clerk of the district court in the county which issued the marriage license.

Must the Celebrant keep records?

The Celebrant is not required to keep records of marriages.

Mississippi

Where do couples apply for a license?

Circuit Clerk's Office

What are the age requirements?

In the event that the female applicant shall be under the age of 21 years of age, and s a resident of the State of Mississippi, the application of marriage shall be made to the Circuit Clerk of the county of residence of the parent or legal guardian of such female applicant.

If either applicant is under 21 years of age, parental consent is needed. If the parent does not accompany the applicant to the office when applying, the Clerk shall send notice of filing the application via certified mail to the parents or legal guardian.

Marriage licenses cannot be issued unless the MALE applicant is at least 17 years of age, and the female applicant is at least 15 years of age.

How much does a license cost?

The marriage license fee is $21+ in cash.

What documents are needed?

You will need:

Full names and addresses of both parties.

Names and addresses of the parents of both parties applying (maiden name of Mother)

Age, Date of Birth, and State of Birth (or Foreign County)

Proof of Age (Driver's License, Birth Certificate, School Record, etc.)

Highest Grade Completed in School

Are there residency requirements?

No.

Is there a waiting period?

No.

How long is a license valid?

90 Days.

Where is a license valid for use?

The State of Mississippi.

What if someone has been married previously?

You will need to show:

The number of previous marriages.

How the last marriage ended.

Date last marriage ended (Bring proof of divorce, if if was within the last six months).

Are there any required tests?

No.

Are proxy marriages allowed?

No.

Can cousins marry?

No.

Are common law marriages recognized?

No.

Are same sex marriages legal?

Yes.

How are the documents returned?

Ministers must send a certificate of marriage to the clerk who issued the marriage license within three months after the marriage.

Must the Celebrant keep records?

The Celebrant is not required to keep records of marriages.

Missouri

Where do couples apply for a license?

The Recorder of Deeds

What are the age requirements?

A person under the age of 18 cannot marry without the consent of the custodial parent or guardian.

A person under age 15 cannot marry without approval of a judge in the county where the marriage license is sought. The statute states that the judge should grant approval only upon a showing of "good cause" and that unusual conditions make the marriage "advisable". Persons lacking mental capacity to consent to marriage cannot marry without court approval.

How much does a license cost?

$58+

What documents are needed?

Picture ID such as Drivers License, and Social Security Card.

Are there residency requirements?

No.

Is there a waiting period?

No.

How long is a license valid?

30 Days. (Confirm this as a few counties may have an expiry of 15 days)

Where is a license valid for use?

The State of Missouri.

What if someone has been married previously?

If you were previously married, the date of your divorce or the date of your spouse's death must be provided. Applicants must wait at least 30 days after the divorce has been finalized before applying for a marriage license. If necessary, a copy of your divorce records or spouse's death certificate can be ordered from your local vital records office and mailed to you.

Are there any required tests?

No.

Are proxy marriages allowed?

Yes.

Can cousins marry?

No.

Are common law marriages recognized?

No.

Are same sex marriages legal?

No.

How are the documents returned?

They must give the couple a marriage certificate and must complete the marriage license and return it to the recorder of deeds within 90 days after the marriage license was issued.

Must the Celebrant keep records?

Ministers must keep a record of all marriages they perform.

Montana

Where do couples apply for a license?

Clerk of the District Court.

If both parties are non-residents of Montana, obtain the license application from the Clerk in the county in which the ceremony will be performed. If one party is a non-resident, his/her part can be sworn to or affirmed in the county and state in which he/she resides.

What are the age requirements?

If you are 16 or 17 years old, you must have the consent of both parents unless only one parent has legal custody of you. Proof of age must be in the form of a certified copy of your birth certificate. Both of you, as a couple, will also have to attend at least two counseling sessions that are at least 10 days apart. This has to be done with a designated counselor who will then have to provide a letter that states the names of the couple, their ages, the dates of the counseling sessions, and what the counselor thinks about their possible marriage. Then judicial consent signed by a district court judge must be given for the Clerk of court's office to issue a marriage license. No one 15 years of age or younger may marry in Montana.

No one 15 years of age or younger may marry in Montana.

How much does a license cost?

$53. Cash Only.

What documents are needed?

Certified copies of birth certificates, blood test waiver (form available in the Clerk's office) and certified copies of divorce decrees. If your birth certificate is from a foreign country, the Clerk's office will need a certified copy of the certificate. It must then be translated to English, by a person authorized to do so, and their signature must be notarized.

Are there residency requirements?

No.

Is there a waiting period?

No waiting period unless under the age of 18.

How long is a license valid?

30 Days.

Where is a license valid for use?

The State of Montana

What if someone has been married previously?

A certified copy of the divorce decree is required.

Are there any required tests?

As of October 1, 2007, a rubella blood test is no longer required for a bride between the ages of 18 and 50. The parties may sign an Informed Consent/Waiver of Requirement of Blood Test form. This form is available at the Clerk of District Court's Office or online at the MT Dept. of Public Health & Human Services website. If you obtain the form from a source other than the Clerk of District Court, please bring the form with you when applying for your marriage license. If the bride is over the age of 50, no waiver is required.

Those persons desiring to consummate a marriage by written declaration without solemnization must secure the premarital blood test waiver (available in the Clerk's office) for the female prior to executing the declaration (40-1-311 through 313 & 40-1-323).

Are proxy marriages allowed?

Yes.

Can cousins marry?

No.

Are common law marriages recognized?

Yes.

Are same sex marriages legal?

Yes.

How are the documents returned?

Ministers must complete and return a marriage certificate to the clerk of the district court within 30 days after the marriage. Also the minister must provide marriage certificates to the bride and groom upon request.

Must the Celebrant keep records?

The Celebrant is not required to keep records of marriages.

Nebraska

Where do couples apply for a license?

County Clerk / Comptroller's Office.

What are the age requirements?

Any person who is at least 19 years old may apply for a marriage license without consent.

Any minor who is 17 or 18 years old may apply for a marriage license with a parental or legal guardian consent. The consent form must be notarized.

If either applicant is under 17 years of age, a license cannot be issued in the State of Nebraska.

How much does a license cost?

$15.00

What documents are needed?

Proof of Identity / Age: Valid driver's license, passport or birth certificate. If a birth certificate is used it must be a certified copy.

Social Security numbers of both bride and groom are requested on the marriage license application.

Applicants must supply the names of their parents (including mother's maiden name), and their parents' birthplaces (city and state or foreign country).

Are there residency requirements?

No.

Is there a waiting period?

No.

How long is a license valid?

1 Year.

Where is a license valid for use?

The State of Nebraska.

What if someone has been married previously?

If either applicant has been married previously, the date the previous marriage ended will be requested (court date or date of death). A copy of the divorce decree or death certificate is not required.

Are there any required tests?

No.

Are proxy marriages allowed?

No.

Can cousins marry?

No.

Are common law marriages recognized?

No.

Are same sex marriages legal?

No.

How are the documents returned?

Ministers must report marriages they perform to the county judge who issued the marriage license within 15 days after the marriage. Also the minister must provide marriage certificates to the bride and groom upon request.

Must the Celebrant keep records?

The Celebrant is not required to keep records of marriages.

Nevada

Where do couples apply for a license?

County Clerk or Recorder.

What are the age requirements?

If you are 16 or 17 years old, you must have one parent or legal guardian present. A notarized written permission is also acceptable. It must be written in English and needs to state the name, birth date, age of the minor child, along with the relationship of the person giving consent. The notary must note that the parent or guardian personally appeared before or was subscribed and sworn to.

If you are under 16, marriage can be authorized only by court order when the request has been filed by either parent or legal guardian.

How much does a license cost?

$35 - $65 depending on county.

What documents are needed?

Valid picture identification. Acceptable identification includes valid Driver's license, valid Identification Card from DMV, valid Passport, Resident Alien card, Military ID, or Certified or original Birth Certificate.

If a foreign birth certificate, it must be translated into English and notarized.

You also need to know you Social Security number.

Are there residency requirements?

No.

Is there a waiting period?

No.

How long is a license valid?

1 Year.

Where is a license valid for use?

The State of Nevada.

What if someone has been married previously?

If you were previously married, your divorce must be final. You need to know the date of your divorce and the location where you were divorced.

Are there any required tests?

No.

Are proxy marriages allowed?

No.

Can cousins marry?

Not nearer of kin than second cousins or cousins of half blood.

Are common law marriages recognized?

No.

Are same sex marriages legal?

Yes.

How are the documents returned?

Ministers must report marriages they perform to the county judge who issued the marriage license within 15 days after the marriage. Also the minister must provide marriage certificates to the bride and groom upon request.

Must the Celebrant keep records?

The Celebrant is not required to keep records of marriages.

New Hampshire

Where do couples apply for a license?

City or Town Clerk

What are the age requirements?

Applicants 18 and over can marry without parental consent.

Non-residents under the age of 18 may not marry in New Hampshire.

No female below the age of 13 or male below the age of 14 may be married in New Hampshire under any conditions.

Female applicants between the ages of 13 and 17 and male applicants between the ages of 14 and 17 can only be married with a waiver and permission from their parent or legal guardian.

How much does a license cost?

$45. Be prepared to pay cash or check. Marriage certificates cost $15.

What documents are needed?

Valid picture identification (with Date of Birth). Acceptable forms of identification include:

 - Valid driver's license or identification card from Department of Motor Vehicles.

 - Valid Passport

 - Valid Military card

Original or certified birth certificate (Foreign birth certificates must be translated into English and notarized).

Applicants should be prepared to furnish their social security number.

Are there residency requirements?

No.

Is there a waiting period?

No.

How long is a license valid?

90 Days.

Where is a license valid for use?

The State of New Hampshire.

What if someone has been married previously?

A certified copy of a death certificate of a former spouse, if applicant is widowed; a certified copy of a final divorce decree, if the applicant is divorced; a certified copy of an annulment decree, if the applicant's previous marriage was annulled. Note: This must be a certified copy of the decree. If your decree has an official seal and the judges signature this may be taken in lieu of a certified decree.

Are there any required tests?

No.

Are proxy marriages allowed?

No.

Can cousins marry?

No.

Are common law marriages recognized?

No.

Are same sex marriages legal?

Yes. (As of January 2015 New Hampshire will recognize same gender marriages from other states).

How are the documents returned?

Ministers must send a copy of the marriage license to the town clerk within six days.

Must the Celebrant keep records?

The Celebrant is not required to keep records of marriages.

New Jersey

Where do couples apply for a license?

Local Registrar.

The marriage license application is to be made in the New Jersey municipality in which either party resides and the license is valid throughout the State of New Jersey.

If neither applicant is a New Jersey resident, submit the application in the municipality where the marriage ceremony will be performed. Such license is only valid in the issuing municipality.

What are the age requirements?

If you are under 18 years of age, you will need both parents to give consent in front of two witnesses in order for you to receive a marriage license. Those under 16 need judicial approval. In the case of pregnancy or the birth of a child, special provisions may apply.

How much does a license cost?

$28. Cash only in some locales.

What documents are needed?

Picture ID such as Drivers License, and certified copies of birth certificates, or naturalization certificates, or valid passports or alien cards. US citizens also need to know their Social Security numbers.

Are there residency requirements?

No.

Is there a waiting period?

There is a mandatory 3 day waiting period before your license is issued to you. In most states, the waiting period does not include Saturdays, Sundays or federal holidays. In some instances, the day the application is filed is not included within the waiting period timeline.

How long is a license valid?

30 Days.

Where is a license valid for use?

The State of New Jersey.

If neither applicant is a New Jersey resident, submit the application in the municipality where the marriage ceremony will be performed. Such license is only valid in the issuing municipality.

What if someone has been married previously?

If you were previously married, the date of your divorce or the date of your spouse's death must be provided. Bring a certified copy of the divorce decree or death certificate. If necessary, a copy of your divorce records or spouse's death certificate can be ordered from your local vital records office and mailed to you.

Are there any required tests?

No.

Are proxy marriages allowed?

No.

Can cousins marry?

Yes.

Are common law marriages recognized?

No.

Are same sex marriages legal?

Yes.

How are the documents returned?

The individual performing the ceremony should file the license with the registrar in the municipality where the marriage took place within 5 days of the wedding.

Must the Celebrant keep records?

The Celebrant is not required to keep records of marriages.

New Mexico

Where do couples apply for a license?

County Clerk's Office.

What are the age requirements?

If the applicant is 16 or 17, parental consent is required.

If the applicant is 15 years of age a court order is required.

How much does a license cost?

$25+. Cash only.

What documents are needed?

A legal picture ID, or birth certificate.

Proof of Social Security number.

Couples living in foreign countries need a passport.

Are there residency requirements?

No.

Is there a waiting period?

No.

How long is a license valid?

1 Year.

Where is a license valid for use?

The State of New Mexico.

What if someone has been married previously?

If previously married, the date of divorce or date of spouse's death must be supplied.

Are there any required tests?

No.

Are proxy marriages allowed?

No.

Can cousins marry?

Yes.

Are common law marriages recognized?

No.

Are same sex marriages legal?

Yes.

How are the documents returned?

Ministers must provide the county clerk with a marriage certificate within 90 days after the marriage.

Must the Celebrant keep records?

The Celebrant is not required to keep records of marriages.

New York

Where do couples apply for a license?

The Town or City Clerk.

What are the age requirements?

If either you or your prospective spouse is under the age of 16 years, you are required to have written parental consent to obtain a Marriage License.

You will need a government issued photo ID.

Please be prepared to show proof of your date of birth. You may show one of the following forms of identification to prove your age:

original or certified copy of birth certificate,

baptismal record,

passport,

driver license,

naturalization record, or

court records.

Both of your parents must be present to consent and have proper identification at the time of application for the Marriage License and at the Marriage Ceremony if the ceremony is performed in our offices.

If one parent is deceased, the surviving parent must appear and a death certificate for the deceased parent must be produced.

If both parents are deceased, the legal guardian must appear instead and show proof of legal guardianship.

If either prospective spouse is under the age of sixteen years, in addition to parental consent, the written approval of a Judge of the Supreme Court or Family Court is needed.

A person under the age of fourteen years cannot be married.

How much does a license cost?

$40 outside of New York City limits or $35 in NYC.

What documents are needed?

The application is an affidavit where you and your prospective spouse must list your name; current address; city, state, ZIP code and country; country of birth; date of birth; name and country of birth of your parents; Social Security number; and marital history.

When you sign the affidavit, you are making a sworn statement that there are no legal impediments to the marriage.

Eight forms of identification are accepted. Expired identification is not accepted.

Driver License with photograph (from the United States of America or any of its territories)

Non-Driver Identification Card with photograph (from the United States of America or any of its territories)

Learner Permit with photograph (from the United States of America or any of its territories)

Active United States Military Identification Card

Passport

United States Certificate of Naturalization (good for 10 years after date of issue)

United States Permanent Resident Card

United States Employment Authorization Card

Are there residency requirements?

No.

Is there a waiting period?

Yes. A 24 hour waiting period after you and your prospective spouse obtain your license is required by New York State Law.

If you and your prospective spouse must marry before the 24 hour waiting period is over, you can request a Judicial Waiver from the County Clerk in the county (borough) where you obtained your Marriage License.

When both applicants are 16 years of age or older, the 24-hour waiting period may be waived by an order of a justice of the Supreme Court or a judge of the County Court of the county (borough) which either of the applicants resides.

If either person is under 16 years of age, the order must be from the Family Court judge of the county (borough) in which the person under 16 years of age resides.

How long is a license valid?

60 Days.

Where is a license valid for use?

New York State.

What if someone has been married previously?

If you were married before, you must list all prior marriages. You must include your previous spouse's full name; the date the divorce decree was granted; and the city, state, and country where the divorce was issued.

All divorces, annulments, and dissolutions must be finalized before you apply for a new Marriage License.

You may be asked to produce the final divorce decree.

If your spouse is deceased, you must provide such spouse's full name and date of death.

Documents must be originals or certified copies.

Are there any required tests?

No.

Are proxy marriages allowed?

No.

Can cousins marry?

No.

Are common law marriages recognized?

No.

Are same sex marriages legal?

Yes.

How are the documents returned?

Ministers must complete a marriage license and return it to the town or city clerk who issued the marriage license within 5 days after the marriage.

Must the Celebrant keep records?

The Celebrant is not required to keep records of marriages.

North Carolina

Where do couples apply for a license?

Register of Deeds

What are the age requirements?

All applicants, including those not present, must provide a form of identification.

Applicants 21 and over may use a valid driver's license, valid Military I.D, State ID, passport or certified birth certificate.

Applicants 18 to 21 must present a certified copy of their birth certificate.

Applicants 16 and 17 must present a consent form signed by the parent, individual, agency or institution having legal custody or serving as the legal guardian of the underage party. A certified copy of the birth certificate is also required. The consent form must be notarized.

Applicants 14 and 15 must provide a certified copy of the court order authorizing the marriage. A certified copy of the birth certificate is also required.

A marriage license may not be issued to applicants under 14 years of age.

How much does a license cost?

$60. ($10 for a copy of the marriage certificate which can be pre-ordered)

What documents are needed?

Proof of Social Security number. Either the Social Security card, a 1040 or W2.

A current and valid government issued photo ID, such as a driver's license, passport, etc.

Are there residency requirements?

No.

Is there a waiting period?

No.

How long is a license valid?

60 Days.

Where is a license valid for use?

The State of North Carolina.

What if someone has been married previously?

If either the bride or groom has been divorced, he or she must know the month and year of the last divorce. If there has been a divorce within the last 60 days, the state requires a copy of the divorce decree signed by the judge.

Are there any required tests?

No.

Are proxy marriages allowed?

No.

Can cousins marry?

Yes. (Not first)

Are common law marriages recognized?

No.

Are same sex marriages legal?

Yes.

How are the documents returned?

Ministers must complete the marriage license and return it to the register of deeds that issued it within 10 days or incur a $200 fine.

Must the Celebrant keep records?

The Celebrant is not required to keep records of marriages.

North Dakota

Where do couples apply for a license?

Register of Deeds

What are the age requirements?

If a person is between 16 and 18 years of age, a marriage license may not be issued without the consent of the parents or guardian. This requires a notarized statement.

A marriage license may not be issued to any person below the age of 16, notwithstanding the consent of the parents or guardian of said person.

How much does a license cost?

$65. Some counties require cash only.

What documents are needed?

Picture ID is required of each. Drivers License or certified copy of Birth Certificate.

Are there residency requirements?

No.

Is there a waiting period?

No.

How long is a license valid?

60 Days.

Where is a license valid for use?

The State of North Dakota

What if someone has been married previously?

If divorced, state law requires that they receive a certified copy of the Divorce Decree to keep with the Marriage License Application.

If widowed, law requires that they receive a plain copy of the Death Certificate of the deceased spouse.

Are there any required tests?

No.

Are proxy marriages allowed?

No.

Can cousins marry?

No.

Are common law marriages recognized?

No.

Are same sex marriages legal?

No.

How are the documents returned?

Ministers must file a certificate of marriage with the county judge who issued the license within 5 days after the marriage. Certificates must also be given to the persons married.

Must the Celebrant keep records?

The Celebrant is not required to keep records of marriages.

Ohio

Where do couples apply for a license?

Probate Court. You must apply in the county in which you want to get married.

What are the age requirements?

If you are 18 to 21 years of age, you will need to show your birth certificate. Persons aged 16-17 must have consent to marry from parents or legal guardians and may have to contact the Probate Court. Additionally, the Jude ay require the minors to state that they have received marriage counseling that is satisfactory to the court.

How much does a license cost?

$40+ depending on county.

What documents are needed?

Government issued ID such as drivers license, visa, passport, state ID. You need to know your social security numbers.

Are there residency requirements?

No.

Is there a waiting period?

No.

How long is a license valid?

60 Days.

Where is a license valid for use?

The State of Ohio.

What if someone has been married previously?

Bring certified copy of divorce decree or a copy of deceased spouse's death certificate.

Are there any required tests?

No.

Are proxy marriages allowed?

No.

Can cousins marry?

No.

Are common law marriages recognized?

Yes.

Are same sex marriages legal?

No.

How are the documents returned?

Ministers must send a certificate of marriage to the probate judge of the county which issued the marriage license within 30 days after the marriage.

Must the Celebrant keep records?

The Celebrant is not required to keep records of marriages.

Oklahoma

Where do couples apply for a license?

The County Clerk.

What are the age requirements?

If under 18 your parents must appear at the courthouse with the couple to sign a consent form. Minors must wait three days before the marriage license is valid.

How much does a license cost?

$50. However, you can have this reduced to only $5 by completing an eligible premarital counseling program such as those offered by The Oklahoma Marriage Initiative.

What documents are needed?

Drivers License, certified birth certificate, passport or his or her Social Security number.

Are there residency requirements?

No.

Is there a waiting period?

No. However, minors must wait three days before the marriage license is valid.

How long is a license valid?

10 Days.

Where is a license valid for use?

The State of Oklahoma.

What if someone has been married previously?

Bring certified copy of divorce decree or a copy of deceased spouse's death certificate.

Are there any required tests?

No.

Are proxy marriages allowed?

No.

Can cousins marry?

No.

Are common law marriages recognized?

Yes.

Are same sex marriages legal?

Yes.

How are the documents returned?

Ministers must complete a certificate of marriage and return it to the clerk or judge who issued the marriage license.

Must the Celebrant keep records?

The Celebrant is not required to keep records of marriages.

Oregon

Where do couples apply for a license?

County Clerk's Office.

What are the age requirements?

Legal marriage is 18.

Anyone not yet 17 years of age cannot legally be married in the State of Oregon. A 17 year old can be married if they have the parent's or guardian's consent.

How much does a license cost?

Between $50 and $60. Cash only.

What documents are needed?

Drivers license or certified birth certificate or passport and his or her Social Security number.

Are there residency requirements?

No.

Is there a waiting period?

3 Days from issue to use.

How long is a license valid?

60 Days.

Where is a license valid for use?

The State of Oregon.

What if someone has been married previously?

A license can be issued one day after the final date of a divorce. The final divorce date is required on the marriage license application.

Are there any required tests?

No.

Are proxy marriages allowed?

No.

Can cousins marry?

No.

Are common law marriages recognized?

No.

Are same sex marriages legal?

Yes.

How are the documents returned?

The minister must send a marriage certificate to the county clerk who issued the marriage license within one month after the marriage.

Must the Celebrant keep records?

The Celebrant is not required to keep records of marriages.

Pennsylvania

Where do couples apply for a license?

Recorder of Deeds or Register of Wills.

What are the age requirements?

A person must be at least 18 years old in order to get married without consent of an adult.

A child who is 16 or 17 can get married with the consent of a parent.

A child under 16 can get married with the consent of a judge and a parent.

How much does a license cost?

Varies from county to county. Please call to confirm.

What documents are needed?

A valid drivers license or official government issued photo identification as well as proof of Social Security number.

Are there residency requirements?

No.

Is there a waiting period?

3 Days.

How long is a license valid?

60 Days.

Where is a license valid for use?

The State of Pennsylvania.

What if someone has been married previously?

If either party has been previously married, he or she must also bring proof that the previous marriage has ended, such as a divorce decree or the date on which the former spouse died, if a widower. If the document is in a language other than English it must be translated. If maiden name is re-adopted you may need to supply a Resumption of Maiden Name.

Are there any required tests?

No.

Are proxy marriages allowed?

No.

Can cousins marry?

No, down to first cousins.

Are common law marriages recognized?

No.

Are same sex marriages legal?

Yes.

How are the documents returned?

The marriage document is in two parts. Ministers must provide a certificate of marriage to the bride and groom. Also, they must send a marriage certificate to the clerk of the orphans' court who issued the marriage license within 10 days after the marriage.

Must the Celebrant keep records?

The Celebrant is not required to keep records of marriages.

Rhode Island

Where do couples apply for a license?

Town Clerk

For Residents:

For marriages, if the bride lives in Rhode Island, the couple should apply for the license at the clerk office in the city or town of the bride's residence. If only the groom lives in Rhode Island, the couple should apply for the license at the clerk office in the city or town of the groom's residence.

For civil unions, if either partner lives in Rhode Island, the couple should apply for the license at the clerk office in the city or town of residence of either of the individual(s).

If at least one partner lives in Rhode Island, the marriage or civil union license is valid in any city or town and the ceremony may take place anywhere in Rhode Island.

For Non-Residents:

If neither partner lives in Rhode Island, the license must be obtained at the clerk office in the city/town where the ceremony will take place. If the ceremony is performed in a city or town other than where it was issued, the validity of the marriage or civil union may be in question.

What are the age requirements?

For marriages where the bride is younger than 18 or if either individual is under the control of a legal guardian, a "Minor's Permit to Marry" must be completed by the parent or legal guardian. Please note that men younger than 18 and women younger than 16 also need a court permission to marry.

Individuals must be at least 18 years of age to form a civil union.

How much does a license cost?

$24

What documents are needed?

Proof of birth facts and a valid form of identification.

Are there residency requirements?

No.

Is there a waiting period?

No.

How long is a license valid?

90 Days.

Where is a license valid for use?

The State of Rhode Island.

What if someone has been married previously?

If previously married or in a civil union, a certified copy of the final decree of divorce or dissolution of the civil union (with the raised or original stamped court seal), or a certified copy of the death certificate of the previous spouse / partner.

Are there any required tests?

No.

Are proxy marriages allowed?

No.

Can cousins marry?

Yes. A man cannot marry his aunt, but can marry his cousin. A woman, by the way, may marry her uncle providing she is Jewish.

Are common law marriages recognized?

Yes.

Are same sex marriages legal?

Yes.

How are the documents returned?

Ministers must endorse and return the marriage license to the town or city clerk in which the marriage was performed.

Must the Celebrant keep records?

The Celebrant is not required to keep records of marriages.

South Carolina

Where do couples apply for a license?

Probate Court.

What are the age requirements?

If you are under the age of 18, parental consent can be granted for boys who are at least 16 years old and for girls who are at least 14 years old. All minor applicants must file an original birth certificate or a certified copy of their birth certificate, which becomes a part of their permanent application record. The parent or legal guardian of a minor applicant must appear at the same time as the minor to present identification and sign a form consenting to the marriage.

If you are 18 years old or older, you do not need parental consent. But you must provide proof of your age (or simply identification if you're over age 25) by presenting one of the following:

Valid driver's license;

Original birth certificate or a certified copy of your birth certificate;

Valid South Carolina identification card issued by the South Carolina Department of Public Safety;   Current military identification card;

Current passport.

How much does a license cost?

Varies from county to county. Please check with the appropriate probate court. Some locales charge extra for out-of-state residents.

What documents are needed?

Drivers License or other valid government ID and Social Security card or other proof of social security number..

Are there residency requirements?

No.

Is there a waiting period?

There is a 24-hour waiting period after the application is filed before the license can be picked up and the marriage can take place. If you want to get married on a weekend, make sure you apply for a marriage license by Thursday so you can pick up your license by Friday.

How long is a license valid?

No expiration date.

Where is a license valid for use?

The State of South Carolina.

What if someone has been married previously?

No proof of divorce is required.

Are there any required tests?

No.

Are proxy marriages allowed?

No.

Can cousins marry?

Yes.

Are common law marriages recognized?

Yes.

Are same sex marriages legal?

Yes.

How are the documents returned?

Ministers must complete the marriage license and give one copy to the parties and the other two must be returned to the county judge of probate who issued it within 15 days after the marriage.

Must the Celebrant keep records?

The Celebrant is not required to keep records of marriages.

South Dakota

Where do couples apply for a license?

Register of Deeds.

What are the age requirements?

Applicants 16 and 17 must have parental consent. South Dakota law does not permit marriage of those under 16.

How much does a license cost?

$40

What documents are needed?

Drivers License or a certified copy of a birth certificate.

Are there residency requirements?

No.

Is there a waiting period?

No.

How long is a license valid?

20 Days.

Where is a license valid for use?

The State of South Dakota

What if someone has been married previously?

Proof of divorce may be required.

Are there any required tests?

No.

Are proxy marriages allowed?

No.

Can cousins marry?

No.

Are common law marriages recognized?

No.

Are same sex marriages legal?

No.

How are the documents returned?

The minister must send a marriage certificate to the clerk who issued the marriage license within 30 days after the marriage.

Must the Celebrant keep records?

Ministers must also keep a record book of all marriages they perform.

Tennessee

Where do couples apply for a license?

County Clerk

What are the age requirements?

If 16 or 17 years of age the parent or guardian must accompany in applying for license.

Custodial parent must bring custody papers (if applicable) to show proof of custody.

If 15 years of age or younger court consent must also be granted before license may be issued.

How much does a license cost?

$93.50 - $99.50. Costs vary from county to county.

It is possible to receive a discount of $60.00. In order to do so, you must complete a premarital preparation course in the year prior to your application date. You will need to provide a Certificate of Completion in order to receive your discount.

According to Tennessee Statutes, non-residents in some counties can receive a $60 discount upon showing the county clerk proof that they are not Tennessee residents.

What documents are needed?

Proof of Social Security number plus one of the following:

State certified birth certificate

Drivers License

State issued ID

For Legal Aliens who do not have a social security number:

Passport and American Visa or Resident Alien Card.

Please know the following:

Parents full name (including maiden name of mother)

Parents state of birth and address (if living)

Applicant's number of prior marriages

Date last marriage ended (if applicable)

Are there residency requirements?

No.

Is there a waiting period?

An underage application includes a 3 day waiting period, but may be waived by a Court of Record or the County Mayor.

How long is a license valid?

30 Days.

Where is a license valid for use?

The State of Tennessee.

What if someone has been married previously?

If previously married you will need to give the number of previous marriages and the date the last marriage ended.

Are there any required tests?

No.

Are proxy marriages allowed?

No.

Can cousins marry?

Yes.

Are common law marriages recognized?

No.

Are same sex marriages legal?

No.

How are the documents returned?

Ministers must endorse the marriage license and return it to the clerk of the county court within three days after the marriage.

Must the Celebrant keep records?

The Celebrant is not required to keep records of marriages.

Texas

Where do couples apply for a license?

The County Clerk.

What are the age requirements?

If you are between 16 and 17 years old, you may apply for a marriage license only if you have written parental consent on an official form in the presence of the county clerk or if you have received an order from the Texas district court authorizing your marriage.

How much does a license cost?

$31 - $71. Cash only. Fees may vary from county to county.

The license fee may be waived if a couple takes an 8 hour premarital preparation course that covers important marital skills and issues such as conflict management and communication.

What documents are needed?

One valid form of ID such as drivers license, certified copy of your birth certificate, US Passport, military ID card.

Your Social Security number.

Are there residency requirements?

No.

Is there a waiting period?

72 hours. This can be waived for active duty military personnel.

How long is a license valid?

30 Days.

Where is a license valid for use?

The State of Texas.

What if someone has been married previously?

If divorced within 30 days, Texas requires that you show a certified copy of your divorce decree stating the 30 day waiting period is waived.

Are there any required tests?

No.

Are proxy marriages allowed?

Yes.

Can cousins marry?

No.

Are common law marriages recognized?

Yes.

Are same sex marriages legal?

No.

How are the documents returned?

Ministers must complete the marriage license and return it to the county clerk who issued it within 30 days after the marriage.

Must the Celebrant keep records?

The Celebrant is not required to keep records of marriages.

Utah

Where do couples apply for a license?

The County Recorder.

What are the age requirements?

You must be at least 15 years old to be married in Utah. If you are over 18, you do not need consent to get married. If you are 16 or 17, you need signed consent from a parent or guardian, which must be given in person to the county clerk before a marriage license will be issued.

If you are 15 years old, you need consent from a parent or guardian, and:

The juvenile court must approve the marriage, and must conclude that the marriage is voluntary and in the best interests of the minor.

The juvenile court may require premarital counseling.

The juvenile court may impose other conditions, such as requiring the minor to continue to attend school.

If you are under 18 but you have been married before, you do not need consent a second time.

How much does a license cost?

$45+ in most counties.

What documents are needed?

Valid picture ID such as a passport, birth certificate, drivers license, or state ID card.

Either bring your Social Security card or know your Social security number.

If you want to use your maiden name on the license bring a certified copy of your birth certificate or a certified copy of your divorce decree that states name is to be changed to maiden name.

Are there residency requirements?

No.

Is there a waiting period?

No.

How long is a license valid?

30 Days.

Where is a license valid for use?

The State of Utah.

What if someone has been married previously?

If previously married, the date of divorce or date of spouse's death must be provided.

Are there any required tests?

No.

Are proxy marriages allowed?

No.

Can cousins marry?

Yes. If both cousins are over the age of 65, or over the age of 55 and can prove sterility.

Are common law marriages recognized?

Yes.

Are same sex marriages legal?

Yes.

How are the documents returned?

Ministers must provide a certificate of marriage to the county clerk who issued the marriage license within 30 days after the marriage.

Must the Celebrant keep records?

The Celebrant is not required to keep records of marriages.

Vermont

Where do couples apply for a license?

Town Clerk's Office.

What are the age requirements?

If you are at least 16, but under 18, you will need the consent of a parent or guardian. They will need to go with you to the town clerk's office to sign an affidavit giving you permission to marry.

No person under 16 may marry in Vermont.

How much does a license cost?

$45

What documents are needed?

Besides basic information about yourselves (names, towns of residence, places and dates of birth), you must also provide your parents' names, including your mothers' birth (maiden) names, and their places of birth. (Certified copies of your birth certificates can supply most of this information).

A valid government issued photo ID.

Are there residency requirements?

No.

Is there a waiting period?

No.

How long is a license valid?

60 Days.

Where is a license valid for use?

The State of Vermont.

What if someone has been married previously?

If your husband, wife or civil union partner has died, you are free to marry. The clerk will ask the date your spouse or civil union partner died. If you are divorced, you may remarry after the date on which your previous marriage or civil union was legally dissolved. If you are partners in an existing civil union, you are free to marry one another.

Are there any required tests?

No.

Are proxy marriages allowed?

No.

Can cousins marry?

No.

Are common law marriages recognized?

No.

Are same sex marriages legal?

Yes.

How are the documents returned?

After the ceremony, the officiant will complete the license, sign it, and return it to the town clerk's office within 10 days of the ceremony so your marriage may be officially registered.

Must the Celebrant keep records?

The Celebrant is not required to keep records of marriages.

Virginia

Where do couples apply for a license?

Circuit Court Clerk.

What are the age requirements?

The minimum age for marriage in the Commonwealth of Virginia is sixteen (16) years for both the bride and groom; however, if either party is under eighteen (18), consent to the marriage must be given by the father, mother or legal guardian. This may be done in person by the parent or legal guardian before the person issuing the license or by written consent properly sworn to before a notary public. Special provisions are made in Virginia law to allow marriage for under age parties when the female is pregnant and for situations in which under age applicants have no parent or legal guardian. A pregnant bride under age may marry without consent if they are pregnant or have been within the last nine months, have a letter from a doctor to confirm this are a resident.

All applicants under 18 must be resident in the state.

How much does a license cost?

$30

What documents are needed?

Each applicant will need a Photo ID.

Applicants must, under oath, furnish information required to complete the marriage record. These items are material and the applicant may be subject to prosecution for perjury for violation of the portion of the statutes which requires this information. For divorced persons, there is no statutory waiting period before marriage after the divorce is granted unless remarriage is specifically prohibited by a court. In some cases, clerks may require documentary proof of age or termination (and date of termination) of previous marriage.

Are there residency requirements?

No.

Is there a waiting period?

No.

How long is a license valid?

60 days.

Where is a license valid for use?

The State of Virginia.

What if someone has been married previously?

For divorced persons, there is no statutory waiting period before marriage after the divorce is granted unless remarriage is specifically prohibited by a court. In some cases, clerks may require documentary proof of age or termination of previous marriage.

Are there any required tests?

No.

Are proxy marriages allowed?

No.

Can cousins marry?

Yes. (First cousins may marry)

Are common law marriages recognized?

No.

Are same sex marriages legal?

Yes.

How are the documents returned?

Ministers must complete the marriage certificate and return it to the clerk who issued the marriage license within five days after the marriage.

Must the Celebrant keep records?

The Celebrant is not required to keep records of marriages.

Washington

Where do couples apply for a license?

The County Auditor.

What are the age requirements?

Applicants who are 17 years of age must be accompanied by one parent or legal guardian who can provide consent.

Applicants under the age of 17 must obtain permission from the Family Court.

How much does a license cost?

$32 - $62+ depending on the county.

What documents are needed?

You must have a current photo ID.

Are there residency requirements?

No.

Is there a waiting period?

There is a mandatory 3 day waiting period before your license is issued to you. In most states, the waiting period does not include Saturdays, Sundays or federal holidays. In some instances, the day the application is filed is not included within the waiting period timeline.

How long is a license valid?

60 Days.

Where is a license valid for use?

The State of Washington.

What if someone has been married previously?

Proof of divorce from a previous spouse, or death of a spouse, is not required to obtain a marriage license. It is the responsibility of the applicant to ensure that the final decree of divorce is filed before applying for a new marriage license.

Are there any required tests?

No.

Are proxy marriages allowed?

No.

Can cousins marry?

No.

Are common law marriages recognized?

No.

Are same sex marriages legal?

Yes.

How are the documents returned?

Ministers must send two certificates of marriage to the county auditor within 30 days after the marriage.

Must the Celebrant keep records?

The Celebrant is not required to keep records of marriages.

West Virginia

Where do couples apply for a license?

County Clerk's Office.

What are the age requirements?

If either of you are under 18 years of age, you must have the consent (in person) of a parent or guardian. There will be a 3 day waiting period after you apply for the license. There may be special provisions for an underage bride who is pregnant.

How much does a license cost?

$36. Cash only. Fees may vary from county to county.

What documents are needed?

You will need to present photo identification such as your driver's license, state ID, or passport. You will also need to know your parent's full names, including your mother's maiden names, and the states where they were born.

Are there residency requirements?

No. However, if you are a West Virginia resident, you must apply in the county where you live.

Is there a waiting period?

No for those 18 or over. 3 days for those under 18.

How long is a license valid?

60 days.

Where is a license valid for use?

State of West Virginia.

What if someone has been married previously?

Most counties will require documentation to prove a previous marriage has been dissolved either through death or divorce.

Are there any required tests?

No.

Are proxy marriages allowed?

No.

Can cousins marry?

No.

Are common law marriages recognized?

No.

Are same sex marriages legal?

Yes.

How are the documents returned?

Ministers must return the completed marriage license to the county clerk who issued it on or before the fifth day of the month following the marriage.

Must the Celebrant keep records?

The Celebrant is not required to keep records of marriages.

Wisconsin

Where do couples apply for a license?

County Clerk's Office.

What are the age requirements?

If either the bride or groom is 16 or 17 years old, parental permission is required. Parents or guardians are required to sign in the presence of a notary public before a marriage application is processed.

How much does a license cost?

$60 - $135. Fees vary by county. Cash only.

What documents are needed?

You must bring your Social Security Card, show proof of residence (WI Driver's License or WI State ID), show a certified copy of your birth certificate. You must know your parents full names, including mother's maiden name and the correct spelling of their names. Make sure you have the date and place of your marriage ceremony and the name, address and phone number of the officiant.

Are there residency requirements?

At least one of the couple must reside in the county where the application is made for at least 30 days. If both reside out-of-state, the application is made in the county where the ceremony will take place.

Is there a waiting period?

There is a mandatory 6 day waiting period before your license is issued to you. In most states, the waiting period does not include Saturdays, Sundays or federal holidays. In some instances, the day the application is filed is not included within the waiting period timeline. A waiver for the 6 day waiting period may be obtained at the discretion of the County Clerk. The cost of the waiver is $25.00.

How long is a license valid?

30 Days.

Where is a license valid for use?

The State of Wisconsin.

What if someone has been married previously?

You must show proof of a divorce, death or annulment from your most recent marriage. A copy of the judgment of divorce (signed by a judge), legal annulment (signed by a judge) or death certificate is required. In Wisconsin, you need to wait six months after a divorce before remarrying no matter what state the divorce took place in.

Are there any required tests?

No.

Are proxy marriages allowed?

No.

Can cousins marry?

Blood relatives who are first cousins must have proof of sterilization unless the female is 55 years of age or older.

Are common law marriages recognized?

No.

Are same sex marriages legal?

Yes.

How are the documents returned?

Ministers must complete the marriage certificates and give one to the bride and one to the groom. The original must be returned to the register of deed's of the county in which the marriage was performed or if performed in a city, to the city health officer. This must be done within 3 days after the marriage.

Must the Celebrant keep records?

The Celebrant is not required to keep records of marriages.

Wyoming

Where do couples apply for a license?

The County Clerk's Office

What are the age requirements?

Applicants must be at least 18 years old or with written parental consent.

Applicants under 16 years of age can apply only with a court order.

How much does a license cost?

$25. Be prepared to pay cash.

What documents are needed?

Valid driver's license, and have a certified copy of your birth certificate.

Are there residency requirements?

No.

Is there a waiting period?

No.

How long is a license valid?

1 Year.

Where is a license valid for use?

The State of Wyoming.

What if someone has been married previously?

If either applicant has been married before, you may be required to bring Proof of Dissolution.

Are there any required tests?

No.

Are proxy marriages allowed?

No.

Can cousins marry?

No

Are common law marriages recognized?

No.

Are same sex marriages legal?

Yes.

How are the documents returned?

Ministers must give a marriage certificate to the bride and groom upon request and must return a certificate to the county clerk.

Must the Celebrant keep records?

The Celebrant is not required to keep records of marriages.

Appendix C: Glossary of Wedding Terms

Aisle Runner
A long piece of fabric traditionally rolled out before the bridal procession to indicate the arrival of the bride.
All-Inclusive
A flat fee that covers a variety of wedding services. Most often associated with destination weddings at resorts.
Arbor
A shelter of branches under which a couple stands to exchange vows. Can also be made of latticework covered with vines.
Asymmetric
A dress neckline where one shoulder is covered and the other is bare, or a style that begins at the natural waistline and angles down to one side.
Basket Weave
An icing technique that mimics the look of a wicker basket, with piped lines of vertical and horizontal icing crisscrossing.
Biscotti
An Italian cookie often flavored with anise or nuts. Common as a wedding favor because of their long shelf-life. Traditionally oblong-shaped.
Black Tie
A semi-formal dress code; men wear tuxedoes, while women wear cocktail dresses or gowns.
Blackout Dates
Dates unavailable for events, either due to holidays or a venue's lack of availability.
Blended Family
A family where members are not all biologically related. Typically, a result of a marriage when spouses and children from a former relationship or marriage form the family unit.
Block of Rooms
A group of rooms reserved at a hotel for guests, often at a discounted rate. The block is usually held in the couple's name, with guests paying for the reservations themselves.
Blusher Veil
A short veil worn over the bride's face while walking down the aisle that is lifted back to present her to the groom.
Bodice
The portion of a woman's garment that covers the upper part of a woman's body, above the waist.
Body Shapers
An undergarment used to mold the bride's body into a smooth silhouette.
Bon Bon
A type of candy that is covered in fondant or chocolate.
Bridal Boot Camp
A high-intensity workout regime for brides to lose weight and tone up before the wedding.
Brides Room
An area at the ceremony venue for the bride and her attendants to prepare for the wedding in private.
Budget
A list of planned expenses for a wedding that serves as a helpful guide to keep track of spending.
Buffet
A type of dining style where guests line up and either serve themselves or request food from the server.
Burlap Linen
A tablecloth made of or resembling burlap, a material of woven jute or hemp.

Bustle
When a wedding gown's train is gathered below the waist to prevent it from dragging on the floor, often done after the wedding ceremony but before the reception.
Butler Service
A type of catering service where servers offer food and drinks to guests on platters.
Cabana
A hut or a structure draped in fabric, typically found on a beach. Can be a relatively small 4-by-4 foot structure intended for shade or large enough to house an entire reception.
Candelabra
A decorative candlestick that has multiple arms to hold multiple candles. Sometimes used as part of the unity candle lighting ceremony.
Candle Lighters
Members of the wedding party, often older children or young adults, who walk up the aisle with lit candles to light candles for the ceremony.
Capacity Charts
A chart that shows how many people a venue can accommodate.
Cardstock
A type of paper commonly used for wedding invitations. Thicker than normal printing paper and comes in varying colors and textures.
Carving Station
An area manned by catering staff who carve slices of meat, such as prime rib or chicken, in a buffet setting at the request of guests.
Cascade Bouquet
A bouquet style in which the flowers cascade downward from the bride.
Cash Bar
A beverage-service system where wedding guests pay for their drinks.
Cathedral Veil
The most formal of veils, also known as a royal veil. Standard length is 108 inches; the veil extends onto the floor.
Celebrant
An individual who officiates the ceremony. For weddings your Celebrant should be licensed to perform in your state.
Chafing Dish
A large dish that sits over a low flame to keep its contents warm. Popular at buffets.
Champagne Flute
A slim glass with a stem, designed to retain Champagne's carbonation.
Charger Plate
A plate, larger than a dinner plate, that is purely decorative and displays the meal's china.
Chartreuse
A bright yellow-green appropriate for a spring wedding
Chauffeur
A person responsible for driving a vehicle, such as a limo. Often the bridal party is chauffeured to the ceremony.
Chill Table
A table that can be filled with ice, over which food is placed to keep fresh.
Cocktail Hour
A festive gathering where guests mingle as cocktails and hors d'oeuvres are served, typically preceding dinner.
Comb
A decorative hairpiece attached to a comb that slides into the hair.
Common Law Marriage
When two people live together as if they are man and wife without going through the formality of marriage.

Crown
An ornamental, often bejeweled, headpiece that circles the head. Veils can be attached.

Cuban Cigars
A popular cigar for celebrations, rolled from Cuban tobacco leaves.

Day of Planner
A wedding planner enlisted to help only on the day of the wedding to make sure that all parts of the event run smoothly.

Destination Wedding
The term for when an engaged couple travels away from home for the wedding ceremony. A destination wedding may or may not include guests.

Down Payment Registry
A registry where the bride and groom request monetary contributions towards the down payment of a home.

Eggshell Blue
A greenish blue resembling the color of a robin's egg. Also called robin egg blue.

Elbow Veil
A veil that extends to the bride's elbow, typically about 25 inches long.

Elopement
When a couple steals away to get married without notifying friends and family.

Emcee
An individual who moves the wedding reception forward by announcing speakers, songs and dances. Comes from the phrase Master of Ceremonies or MC.

Engagement Party
A party thrown at the beginning of the engagement, sometimes to announce the engagement to friends and family. Traditionally thrown by the bride's family but may be thrown by the couple.

Engagement Session
A series of photos taken by the wedding photographer during the engagement. Often used in wedding announcements, save-the-date cards or at the wedding.

Euro Tie
A long tie with a square bottom that is a cross between a regular necktie and the more formal ascot.

Favor Tags
A decorative label, sticker or hanging tag on a wedding favor. Usually printed with the couple's names or initials and the wedding date.

Final Guarantee
The final head count given to the caterer. The bride and groom will pay for this number.

Finger Sandwich
A small sandwich meant to be eaten in a couple of bites, often part of a buffet.

Fondant
A sweet icing that is rolled out and draped over a wedding cake for a smooth finish.

Food Stations
A style of dinner service that consists of multiple buffets set up at stations throughout the reception location. These stations are often chef-attended and may be themed by food type or cuisine style.

Frame Tent
A type of tent that can be installed without stakes or internal poles; these tents are typically small, no wider than 40 feet.

Full Service Planner
A wedding planner who assists the couple with every step of the wedding process, from selecting vendors to day-of coordination.

Garland
A full circle of flowers. Can be part of decor or worn in the hair.

Gerbera Daisy
A flower from the sunflower family that comes in many different colors; appropriate for a casual, spring wedding. Sometimes called Gerber daisy.

Gobo
A template attached to a light source to create a design, such as a monogram, that shines on the floor, wall or ceiling.

Gown Preservation
The method for preserving a dress after the wedding day. Typically involves a professional cleaning and boxing it to prevent damage over the years.

Green/Eco Wedding
A catchall term that can refer to different aspects of environmentally friendly weddings; can include serving organically grown food, using recyclable items, cutting down on waste, etc.

Groom's Cake
A secondary cake to the traditional wedding cake. Often masculine in design, reflective of the groom's interests or hobbies, and traditionally chocolate.

Head Table
A long, straight table set up for the meal during a reception. Typically the bride and groom sit at the center of the table, facing guests, with the bridal party and their dates flanking the couple.

Hen Party
The term used in some countries for a "bachelorette party," celebrating the last days of a bride-to-be's single life.

Honeymoon Package
A vacation package marketed to honeymooners. Usually includes accommodations and local or romantic activities.

Honeymoon Registry
An online service that allows couples to register for activities and upgrades for their honeymoon stay. This can be used instead of or with more traditional gifts and registries.

Honor Attendant
The attendant the bride wants by her side for the entire wedding process. Also called the maid of honor if the person is unmarried or matron of honor if married.

Hors d'oeuvre
French for "outside of work," referring to a food item served outside of the main body of the meal. Often used interchangeably with the word appetizer.

Hosted Bar
A beverage service system where the host pays for all drinks ordered by the guests. Also known as an open bar.

In-House Catering
Catering services supplied by the wedding venue. If a venue offers in-house catering, typically off-site caterers are not permitted.

In-Law
The parents of a spouse, such as a mother-in-law or father-in-law.

Jewelry Roll
A pouch used to transport jewelry when traveling. Often made of cloth and contains pockets that can be zipped. The pouch is then rolled and secured with an attached ribbon.

Jordan Almond
A candy-coated, often pastel almond that serves as a popular wedding favor.

Junior Bridesmaid
A female who is too old to be a flower girl and too young to be a traditional bridesmaid. Often participates in the bridal shower, ceremony rehearsal, rehearsal dinner and the ceremony processional but not the bachelorette party.

LED
A type of light popular for creating a dramatic event atmosphere; acronym for light-emitting diode.
Locally Grown
Items that are grown near the location they will be used; an encouraged element for eco-friendly weddings.
Luminaria
A decorative lantern most commonly made from a paper bag, then weighted with sand and lit inside with a candle.
Man of Honor
The title of the chief attendant to the bride when he is male.
Map cards
A card sent with the invitation that contains a small map and directions to the wedding ceremony and reception from the places that guests will likely stay.
Marquee Tent
A large tent used in place of a building at outdoor events. Almost always professionally installed.
Marquise
The shape of a diamond that resembles an oval with pointed ends, like a football.
Matron of Honor
The title of the chief bridesmaid when she is married, referred to as "maid of honor" when unmarried.
Micro-Pave
A band with many tiny stones embedded in it, typically set around a larger diamond.
Milgrain Edging
A beaded or textured edge on a wedding band.
Minister
The individual who performs, or administers, your wedding or any other ceremony. A Minister need not be clergy or religiously affiliated but should be licensed to practice and experienced.
Mocktail
A mock cocktail that resembles a drink with spirits but contains no alcohol.
Monogram
The initials of a person's name, often appearing in an ornate, overlapping form and can be used on wedding invitations, piped on cakes as icing, etc.
Nosegay
A small, round bouquet of flowers wired together. Sometimes called a "posy."
Nuptial Blessing
A blessing by a priest occurring at the end of a Roman Catholic wedding ceremony.
Officiant
The person in charge of the wedding ceremony. They must be legally able to marry someone in their state but are not required to be a clergy member.
Online Proofing
An online service that allows a person to review print pieces, such as invitations or photography, before ordering them.
Organic Catering
Catered food grown without the use of pesticides or fertilizers. The food is often sourced from sustainable, local vendors
Organic Flowers
Flowers grown without the use of chemical pesticides.
Pages
A person who holds the train of a bride's gown when she walks down the aisle. This position is usually fulfilled by a boy under the age of 10 but older than the ring bearer.
Palladium
A silver-white pure metal; does not react with oxygen and will not tarnish, unlike silver or gold.

Parure
A matching set of jewelry, such as earrings and a necklace, sometimes intended to be worn at the wedding when presented as a gift by the bride.

Pashmina
A wrap of fine cashmere wool that women drape over their shoulders to keep warm when wearing formal attire.

Personal Vows
When the bride and groom express their commitment to each other with vows they've written rather than recite vows from the Book of Common Prayer.

Petit four
A small, individual cake covered on all sides with fondant.

Pew Vase
A container for flowers that is placed on or by a church pew.

Plantable Favor
A gift for guests that includes seeds, sometimes embedded in paper, that one can plant as a reminder of the wedding.

Playlist
The list of songs given to the DJ or band to play during the reception. Sometimes an iPod is used instead.

Plus-one
A notation on an invitation indicating that a guest can bring a significant other or date.

Prelude
Music played while guests are being seated for the wedding ceremony.

Premarital Counseling
Counseling that the couple receives before the wedding and specific to potential marital issues. Required by some religions before the couple can marry in the church.

Prenuptial Agreement
A contract where a bride and groom agree how property should be divided in the event of death or divorce. Also referred to as a "prenup."

Procession
The order in which the bridal party enters the ceremony. Differs depending on religion or style of ceremony, but generally begins with male attendants, followed by female attendants, and ends with the bride and her escort, if she has one. Or, male and female attendants walk down the aisle side by side, followed by the bride.

Processional
The song played as the bride walks down the aisle, traditionally "The Bridal Chorus" or as it is more commonly known, "The Wedding March."

Proof of Residency
A document that proves residency of a country or state. Can be an electric bill, apartment rental receipt, etc. Often required to obtain a wedding license.

Pub Crawl
A party that travels to different pubs or bars within walking distance on the same night.

Push Pole Tent
A traditional style of tent where a series of poles and stakes hold up the fabric.

R.S.V.P.
A request for invitees to accept or decline an invitation. French for "Répondez s'il vous plaît," meaning "Respond, if you please." An invitee should send an R.S.V.P. whether or not they can attend the event.

Recessional
Music that plays as the bridal party is leaving the ceremony.

Refundable Deposit
Money given to hold a venue or service that will be returned if the event is cancelled due to extenuating circumstances.

Rehearsal Dinner
A tradition, typically held the night before the wedding, where the wedding party celebrates with dinner after practicing for the wedding ceremony.

Response Card
A card accompanying an invitation to a wedding that allows the recipient to accept or decline the invitation. It typically includes meal options. Sometimes called "reply card."

Responsive Vows
Answering "I will" or "I do" to a series of commitment questions asked of the bride and groom by the officiant.

Ring Pillow
A small cushion carried by the ring bearer in the procession. Traditionally holds the rings for delivery to the officiant, but now often holds decorative rings as a representation.

Roast
A type of toast that consists of poking fun at the honoree.

Save-the-date
An announcement of the date of the wedding, requesting guests to "save the date" so they can attend the wedding; sent before the official invitation with the specific details.

Scavenger Hunt
An activity where teams compete against each other to find all the objects on a list.

Seating Cards
Cards propped up at place settings that indicate who sits where during a meal.

Secular Officiant
An official unrelated to a religion who can legally wed two parties, such as a judge.

Sheath
A dress style with a narrow fit that's ankle-length and hugs the bust, waist and hips.

Shoulder Season
Refers to the time between the high and low seasons of travel, often offering lower rates to travelers.

Site Coordinator
A venue staff member who serves as the contact person and coordinator for events in a role that is less extensive than the wedding planner.

Solitaire
A simple metallic band with one stone.

Spray
A single branch or stem with many blooms or leaves on it.

Stag and Doe party
A combined bachelor and bachelorette party.

Stag Party
The term used in some countries for a "bachelor party," celebrating the last days of a groom-to-be's bachelorhood.

Stargazer Lily
A brightly colored, extremely fragrant flower sometimes found in bridal bouquets.

Stepparent
The parent of the child by marriage, not biologically.

String Quartet
A musical ensemble of four musicians playing string instruments, which typically includes two violins, a viola and a cello.

Swagging
A decorative element where fabric is draped to form a curve between two points. Often seen on the skirts of tables or as an effect to create the ceiling of a tent.

Tailcoat
A coat with tails. Seen primarily at weddings with white tie attire. May be a dress coat with a squarely cut away front or a morning coat with a tapered cut.

Tails
The two tapered extensions on the back of a formal tuxedo jacket.

Tension Tent
A parabola-shaped tent with clean lines, capable of withstanding winds up to 70 miles per hour. Contains few internal poles, making it a popular choice for large weddings.

Theme Wedding
A wedding centered around a specific theme that is not color or pattern focused, such as a winter wonderland.

Tiffany Setting
A traditional setting for a solitaire engagement ring that includes a plain band with a set of prongs that holds the diamond. Also called a Tiffany mount.

Toastmaster
The person in charge of introducing speakers and proposing toasts.

Topiary
A sculpture made out of shrubs or flowers. Floral topiaries can make colorful centerpieces.

Tossing Bouquet
A bouquet that is usually smaller than the more formal bouquet the bride carries down the aisle, specifically for throwing to single female guests during the customary bouquet toss.

Traditional Vows
Vows that a bride and groom repeat outloud to each other to express their love and commitment during the wedding ceremony.

Trellis
Latticework, often made of wood or metal, that supports climbing plants. Can provide a decorative backdrop to outdoor weddings.

Tribute Band
A band that plays songs entirely written by a popular band.

Trousseau
Historically refers to the bride's possessions that she brings to the marriage. Can also refer to the bride's gown or attire.

Trunk Show
A presentation of wedding attire, often by a designer, to bridal shops or brides, typically transported in trunks.

Tulle
A light, netted fabric used for veils, wedding gowns and decor.

Unity Candle
A large pillar candle the bride and groom light with two taper candles, symbolizing two individuals committing to each other.

Universal Registry
A single registry where brides and grooms can include gift preferences from many different stores.

Usher
Male bridal party member who show guests to their seats before the ceremony. Often also performs the role of groomsman.

Videographer
The person responsible for filming and editing a video of the wedding ceremony and reception.

VIEs
An acronym for "Very Important Extras," where family and friends can fulfill roles extending beyond the bridal party, from usher to soloist.

Waiting Period
The amount of time legally required between applying for a marriage license and being able to marry. Varies between states.

Wedding Arch
An arched structure commonly used at outdoor weddings that the bride and groom stand under during the ceremony.

Wedding Day Coordinator
A coordinator employed for the day of the wedding only; responsible for the execution of the wedding ceremony and reception.

Wedding Insurance
A policy that prevents financial loss from canceling a wedding due to natural disasters, medical emergencies, etc.

Wedding Planner
An individual an engaged couple hires to oversee every aspect of the wedding, including vendors, payment, decor, budget, etc. The wedding planner is onsite during the event to make sure things run smoothly.

Welcome Basket
A basket filled with items such as candles, guidebooks and other small luxuries, left for out-of-town guests in their hotel room or at the reception desk.

White Tie
The most formal dress attire. For men, this means white bowties and jackets with tails, while women should wear evening gowns. Also called "full evening dress."

Appendix D: Glossary of Funeral and Memorial Terms

Apportionment
This is when the cremated remains are divided into separate amounts. This can be done so some may be spread and the rest retained, or to distribute between members of the family.

Arrangement Conference
The meeting with the funeral director and staff to make the funeral arrangements.

Arrangement Room
A room used to meet with the family and conduct the arrangement conference.

Beneficiary
The person who is the recipient of the proceeds of the will or life insurance policy.

Bequest
Making a gift in a will.

Bereavement / Grief Counselor
Some funeral homes will have a member of staff qualified to provide counseling for bereaved family.

Burial
The act of burying the deceased underground.

Burial / Creation Permit or Certificate
A permit issued by local government that authorizes the burial or cremation.

Burial Garments
Clothes especially made for the deceased.

Burial Vault
The container placed inside the gravesite to hold the casket.

Canopy
A portable canvas shelter or marquee used to cover the gravesite during the burial service.

Casket or Coffin
The container generally made from steel, metal or wood for placing human remains in for burial.

Casket Veil
A transparent net that goes over the casket to keep flies off.

Catafalque
The stand that the casket rests on during a funeral service.

Cemetery
An area of land that is zoned for the burial or entombment of the deceased.

Cenotaph
A monument (sometimes an empty tomb) that is erected in memory of a person buried elsewhere, such as military cenotaphs.

Certified Crematory Operator
If the funeral home has an on-site crematory, they will have a member of staff trained and certified to operate the cremation equipment.

Certified Death Certificate
The legal copy of the original death certificate.

Chapel
A large room used for the purposes of conducting a funeral service.

Codicil
An amendment to a will that supersedes any original provisions.

Columbarium
A building that houses multiple niches.

Committal Service
The final part of the funeral service where the deceased is interred, entombed or cremated.

Community Liaison
This is a newer role in funeral homes and can be held by a member of staff who works to liaise with the community, providing outreach services and education for seniors about funeral planning. It is now an important role to move funeral homes into their changing role in culture in the 21st century.

Contest
The legal challenge to the validity of the will.

Continuing Care Coordinator / After Care
This is a role sometimes held by a member of staff who specifically provides after care service to a family once the funeral is conducted. It can often be the same member of staff who is trained in counseling.

Coroner
A public official whose role it is to investigate the cause of death if no physician was in attendance for a period prior to the death.

Cortege
The funeral procession.

Cosmetology
The use of make-up to enhance the appearance of the deceased.

Cremains
Another term sometimes used for cremated remains.

Cremation
The reduction of the body to ashes with extreme heat.

Cremation Urn
The container that the cremated remains can be stored in.

Crematory / Tort
The machine or furnace designated specifically for the cremation of human remains.

Crypt
A type of vault or room used for holding remains.

Death Notice / Obituary
The formal notice placed in the press that communicates the death and any funeral arrangements.

Deceased
The person who has died.

Disinter
This is when remains are dug up and removed to another place.

Display Room
A room set aside for the purpose of displaying funeral merchandise such as caskets, urns, prayer cards, etc.

Embalmer
The trained and certified person who can disinfect and preserve human remains.

Embalming
The method of preserving and sanitizing the deceased by circulating an antiseptic preservative through the circulatory system.

Eulogy
A speech given at the funeral in honor of the deceased.

Executor
The administrator of the estate, as outlined in the will.

Exhume
To dig up human remains, usually to conduct further tests to determine the cause of death or identity of the deceased.

Family Room
A special room where the bereaved family can convene in privacy.

Final Disposition
The final process for human remains.

Final Rites
The funeral service, can be considered in the faith aspect, rites of passage etc.
First Call
The initial and immediate visit by a funeral director to collect the deceased.
Flower Stand or Rack
Stands used to put floral displays on.
Funeral Arrangements
The conference between family and funeral director to arrange the funeral.
Funeral Assistant
This role is performed by a person not certified as a funeral director or mortician. They provide support services throughout the funeral arranging and funeral service processes.
Funeral Director / Mortician
This is the certified and trained professional who is licensed to perform the supervision and preparation of the deceased for burial or cremation.
Funeral Insurance / Burial Insurance
An insurance policy that covers the costs associated with a funeral or burial.
Funeral Procession
The procession of vehicles between funeral home and church, cemetery or crematory.
Funeral Service
The service or ceremony performed before the final disposition. Can be religious or non-religious.
Grave
The hole in the earth that the deceased is buried in.
Grave Liner
A receptacle made of wood, metal or concrete that lines the grave to give it some integrity.
Grave Marker, Headstone, Memorial Marker or Monument
The above terms all refer to a marker placed upon a grave to identity the occupant of the grave. It can be constructed of marble, granite, stone, wood or other materials.
Green Burial
This refers to a burial conducted without any unnatural materials. i.e. no embalming and a burial in a wooden casket with no metal, or a shroud and buried directly into the earth without a grave liner.
Honorary Pallbearers
Friends or members of a fraternal, military or social organization who may provide a 'honor guard' but do not actually carry the casket.
Inquest
An official hearing if there are circumstances surrounding the cause of death.
Interment
The act of burying a body.
Intestate
When someone dies with no will.
Living Will
A legal document which details the wishes of an individual about his/her medical care should they become unfit to make decisions.
Lowering Device
This is the mechanism used to assist the funeral staff lower the casket into the grave.
Mausoleum
A building that houses above-ground tombs, crypts and niches.
Medical Examiner
Government official whose duty it is to perform an autopsy if one is required.
Memorial Service
A service or ceremony conducted in memory of the deceased, generally without the body present.

Memory Board or Memory Table
A display board where memorabilia about the deceased can be displayed.
Memory Book or Guest Book
A book that attendees can write their condolence messages in and any tribute to the deceased.
Minister's Room
A room for the use of a minister to prepare before a service and/or meet with family.
Morgue
A place where human remains are stored pending an autopsy or an official identification.
Niche
A small space designed to accommodate a cremated remains container.
Obituary
The notice of death published in a newspaper or online.
Opening and Closing Fees
The fees a cemetery charge for digging the grave and filling it, or for opening & closing an existing plot to inter a further occupant, or cremated remains.
Pallbearers
Family and friends who carry the casket during a funeral. This role can be performed by funeral home employees as well.
Perpetual Care Fund
A portion of funds set aside in trust for the ongoing maintenance of a burial plot.
Prayer Cards
Personalized stationery used during a funeral service.
Prearranged Funeral, Funeral Trust, and Preneed
These all refer to plans and contracts which involve preplanning funeral arrangements and prepaying before a death occurs.
Preparation Room
A room specially equipped for the preparation of the deceased. It is ordinarily where embalming, dressing and any cosmetology will take place.
Preplan Advisor / Advance Funeral Planner
This role is performed by a licensed funeral director or licensed preplan agent. They are specifically trained in the role of assisting families with the financial aspects of preplanning a funeral.
Probate
The court process to validate a will.
Reposing Room
The room where the deceased lies in state once casketed and awaiting the time of the funeral service.
Slumber Room
A room that contains a bed for the deceased to be laid in state prior to the funeral. This can be used for viewing or visitation purposes when a casket is not being used. i.e. for a cremation.
Testator
A person making a valid will.
Tomb
A chamber in the ground or above ground in rock or stone that houses human remains.
Trade Embalmer
A licensed embalmer who is not employed in a funeral home but provides embalming services as a trade service to funeral homes.
Transit Permit
The permit issued that enables the deceased to be transported to the burial site.
Trust
A monetary fund that is managed by one person for the benefit of others.

Viewing
When the deceased is laid-out for family and friends to visit before or after a funeral service.
Vigil
A Catholic service held on the eve of a funeral service.
Visitation
This is generally arranged as a private opportunity for family and friends to visit with the deceased before the funeral.
Visitation Room
A room designated in the funeral home for the deceased to lie before the funeral so that people can view the deceased.
Wake
A form of death ritual where a watch is maintained over the deceased during the night before and after the funeral.
Will
A legal document stating the wishes of the deceased in terms of the disposal of their estate and their remains.

Appendix E: Sample Wedding Questionnaire

WEDDING CEREMONY PLANNING QUESTIONNAIRE

COUPLE DETAILS
- NAME OF BRIDE
- BRIDE'S TELEPHONE
- BRIDE'S E-MAIL
- NAME OF GROOM
- GROOM'S TELEPHONE
- GROOM'S E-MAIL

CEREMONY LOCATION DETAILS
- DATE / TIME OF CEREMONY
- CEREMONY LOCATION
- OUTDOORS OR INDOORS?
- VENUE CONTACT
- VENUE TELEPHONE
- APPROX. NUMBER ATTENDING
- IS THERE A REHEARSAL?
- REHEARSAL DETAILS (if applies)

WEDDING PARTY DETAILS
- NO. OF GROOMSMEN
- NO. OF BRIDESMAIDS
- NO. OF RING BEARERS
- NO. OF FLOWERGIRLS
- NAME OF BEST MAN
- NAME OF MD / MT OF HONOR
- BRIDE'S ESCORT DETAILS
- WHO TO HOLD RINGS (if applies)
- WITNESS DETAILS (if applies)

PROFESSIONAL CONTACTS
- WEDDING PLANNER (if applies)
- OTHER VENDER CONTACTS

CONTINUED OVER

WEDDING CEREMONY PLANNING QUESTIONNAIRE (Page 2)

CEREMONY REQUIREMENTS

PROCESSIONAL ORDER

WILL THERE BE A "GIVING AWAY"?

VOWS

RECITED	REPEATED	RESPONSIVE

VOW DETAILS

READINGS

DETAILS OF ANY READINGS AND WHO WILL DELIVER THEM

CEREMONIAL OR UNITY ELEMENTS

DETAILS OF ANY CEREMONIAL ADDITIONS

OTHER DETAILS

WILL YOU EXCHANGE RINGS?

WILL YOU EXCHANGE A KISS?

HOW WOULD YOU LIKE TO BE PRESENTED?

OTHER NOTES

Appendix F: Sample Memorial Questionnaire

MEMORIAL CEREMONY PLANNING QUESTIONNAIRE

MAIN CONTACT DETAILS

- NAME OF CONTACT
- ADDRESS
- TELEPHONE
- E-MAIL

CEREMONY LOCATION DETAILS

- TYPE OF CEREMONY
- DATE / TIME OF CEREMONY
- CEREMONY LOCATION
- OUTDOORS OR INDOORS?
- VENUE CONTACT
- VENUE TELEPHONE
- APPROX. NUMBER ATTENDING

DECEASED'S DETAILS

- NAME
- ADDRESS
- DATE OF BIRTH
- MARITAL STATUS
- NEXT OF KIN
- DATE OF DEATH
- OCCUPATION
- PLACE OF BIRTH
- FAMILY AND OTHER DETAILS

CONTINUED OVER

MEMORIAL CEREMONY PLANNING QUESTIONNAIRE (Page 2)

CEREMONY DETAILS— SPEAKERS AND READINGS

SPEAKER ONE	
SPEAKER ONE DESCRIPTION	
SPEAKER TWO	
SPEAKER TWO DESCRIPTION	
SPEAKER THREE	
SPEAKER THREE DESCRIPTION	
SPEAKER FOUR	
SPEAKER FOUR DESCRIPTION	
SPEAKER FIVE	
SPEAKER FIVE DESCRIPTION	
SPEAKER SIX	
SPEAKER SIX DESCRIPTION	
SPEAKER SEVEN	
SPEAKER SEVEN DESCRIPTION	
SPEAKER EIGHT	
SPEAKER EIGHT DESCRIPTION	
SPEAKER NINE	
SPEAKER NINE DESCRIPTION	
SPEAKER TEN	
SPEAKER TEN DESCRIPTION	

CEREMONY DETAILS— MUSIC AND PERFORMANCE

TITLE ONE	
ARTIST ONE	
TITLE TWO	
ARTIST TWO	
TITLE THREE	
ARTIST THREE	
TITLE FOUR	
ARTIST FOUR	
TITLE FIVE	
ARTIST FIVE	
TITLE SIX	
ARTIST SIX	

MEMORIAL CEREMONY PLANNING QUESTIONNAIRE (Page 3)

SPECIAL CEREMONY COMPONENTS

MEMORIAL DISPLAYS AND ADDITIONS

PREFERRED TRIBUTE

CONTINUED OVER

MEMORIAL CEREMONY PLANNING QUESTIONNAIRE (Page 4)

BIOGRAPHCAL INFORMATION AND NOTES

PRICE QUOTE INFORMATION

AMOUNT FOR PREPARATION	
AMOUNT FOR OFFICIATING	
TRAVEL MILES	
AMOUNT FOR TRAVEL	
TOTAL QUOTED	

Appendix G: Example Contract / Information Form

CONTRACT FOR OFFICIANT SERVICES

CEREMONY DETAILS

TYPE OF CEREMONY

DATE / TIME OF CEREMONY

CEREMONY LOCATION

IS A REHEARSAL REQUIRED?

DATE / TIME OF REHEARSAL

OTHER REQUIREMENTS

COST FOR CEREMONIES

COST FOR TRAVEL EXPENSES

TOTAL FEE

SIGNATURES

By signing below all parties agree that they have, read, agreed to and understand all terms listed overleaf.

SIGNATURE OF CLIENT

PRINT NAME

DATE

SIGNATURE OF SECOND CLIENT

PRINT NAME

DATE

SIGNATURE OF OFFICIANT

PRINT NAME

DATE

CONTINUED OVER

CONTRACT FOR OFFICIANT SERVICES (Page 2)

TERMS AND CONDITIONS

ENTIRE AGREEMENT:
This agreement contains the entire understanding between the Officiant and Client (or clients if a couple).

CONFIRMATION:
A signed "CONTRACT FOR OFFICIANT SERVICES" and payment of the booking fee are necessary to confirm the ceremony preparation and ceremonial services from the Officiant.

SCOPE OF PROVISION:
This contract is solely for the creation and performance of a ceremony (plus rehearsal if listed). The Officiant is not responsible for the provision or supply of venue, furniture, structures, music or any other physical items or contractors required for the event.

PRE-WEDDING CONSULTATION:
The Officiant agrees to provide all required or requested preparation prior to the ceremony. The text and structure of the ceremony should be finalized no later than one week before the date of the wedding.

LIMIT OF LIABILITY:
If the Officiant is too ill, or becomes injured, and cannot supply the services specified above, the Officiant will try to book a replacement officiant. If no officiant is available then liability is limited to a refund of any payments received.

BOOKING FEE/DEPOSIT:
In the event of the client cancelling the ceremony for whatever reason. the booking fee is non refundable. It will be considered as liquidated damages to the Officiant.

REHEARSALS:
A rehearsal is considered an a separate event from the ceremony and therefore an extra charge is billed in addition to the standard fee for creating and performing the ceremony. Where travel costs are incurred for the separate rehearsal event these are in addition to those for the ceremony itself.

FINAL PAYMENT:
All final payments must be made *at least 24 hours* before the performing of the wedding ceremony. We are very happy to accept cash, check or credit card. Checks should made payable as stipulated at time of request.

Appendix H: Further Resources

Online Resources

The Society of Celebrations
http://www.societyofcelebrations.org/

The Humanist Society
http://humanist-society.org/

The Humanist Celebrants Facebook Group
https://www.facebook.com/groups/140217139410738/

The Church of Spiritual Humanism
http://www.spiritualhumanism.org/

The American Association of Wedding Officiants Yahoo Group
https://groups.yahoo.com/neo/groups/weddingofficiants/

Have your Celebrant business listed on WeddingWire.com
http://www.weddingwire.com/vendor/VendorHome

Create a business page for your wedding officiant business on Facebook.
https://www.facebook.com/pages/create/

Create a page for your wedding officiant business at Google+ for business.
https://plus.google.com/pages/create
http://www.google.com/business/

Create an account for your wedding officiant business at Twitter.
https://twitter.com/

Promote your business visually by creating an account for your business with Pinterest.
http://www.pinterest.com/

Add your wedding officiant listing to the directory at Yahoo Local.
https://smallbusiness.yahoo.com/local-listings/

Add your wedding officiant listing to the directory at Yelp.
https://biz.yelp.com/

Join and list yourself in the online professional directory LinkedIn.
https://www.linkedin.com/

Add your wedding business listing at the Bing Business Portal.
https://www.bingplaces.com/

Learn about performing wedding ceremonies by watching videos of wedding ceremonies at YouTube.
http://www.youtube.com/

Find webmaster help and improve your site's visibility in Google search results by using Google Webmaster Tools.
https://www.google.com/webmasters/tools/

 Start a basic Blog.
https://www.blogger.com/

Download free graphics and free printable materials...
http://all-free-download.com/free-vector/vector-wedding-graphics.html

Recommended Reading

Alexander, Becky. The Complete Guide to Baby Naming Ceremonies, How To Books, 2010

Berkun, Scott. Confessions of a Public Speaker, O'Reilly, 2010

Black, Algernon D., Without Burnt Offerings, Ceremonies of Humanism, Viking Press, 1974.

Blum, Marcy. Weddings For Dummies, Hungry Minds, Inc, 1997

Collins, Herrick, and Pearce, ed. Seasons of Life. Prometheus Books, 2000.

Hancock, Jennifer. The Humanist Approach to Grief and Grieving. CreateSpace Independent Publishing Platform 2013.

Lamont, Corliss. A Humanist Funeral Service. Prometheus Books, 1977.

Lamont, Corliss. A Humanist Wedding Service. Prometheus Books, 1972.

Long. Rev. Amy. Weddings, Funerals and Rites of Passage. Self-Published, 2002

Long. Rev. Amy. More Weddings, Funerals and Rites of Passage. Self-Published, 2009

Moore, Faith. Celebrating a Life: Planning Memorial Services and Other Creative Rememberances, Stewart, Tabori & Chang 2009

Morgan, Ernest. Dealing Creatively with Death, Upper Access Books, 2001

The Staff of Entrepreneur Media. Start Your Own Business, Fifth Edition: The Only Start-Up Book You'll Ever Need, Entrepreneur Press; 5th edition (October 2010)

Willson, Jane W, Sharing the Future: Non-religious wedding ceremonies, British Humanist Association, 1988.

Willson, Jane W, New Arrivals: Guide to Nonreligious Naming Ceremonies, Baby naming ceremonies and poetry, published by British Humanist Association, 1991.

Willson, Jane W. Funerals Without God, published by BHA and Prometheus Books, 1995.

Wine, Sherwin. Celebrations: A Ceremonial and Philosophic Guide for Humanists and Humanistic Jews. Prometheus Books, 1988.

York, Sarah. Remembering Well: Rituals for Celebrating Life and Mourning Death. Jossey-Bass, 2000.

Zorger, R. A. The Officiant's Manual. Church of Spiritual Humanism. 2nd Ed.

Afterword

The world of ceremonies is always changing. If you have a suggestion for our next edition, please forward it to us. Additionally, if you think there is a part of this handbook we could improve, we want to hear what you have to say. If you are a practicing Celebrant, enjoy your work. It can be one of the most fulfilling jobs in the world.

Printed in the USA
CPSIA information can be obtained
at www.ICGtesting.com
LVHW070219201223
766983LV00017B/762